The Haçienda

THREADS

The Haçienda

THREADS

A celebration of music,
fashion & friendship

Compiled by
Rebecca Hook

Text by Paul Tierney

Interviews by Emma Davidson

WELBECK

CONTENTS

FAC51
THE HAÇIENDA

1982-1984

1984-1986

1986-1988

1988-1991

1991-1993

1993-1996

The Legacy

Foreword

This book has been a revelation. My memories of the Haçienda have always centred on its famous cockups. No cloakroom, a glass roof, awful sound, bad positioning of the stage and DJ box, the huge costs involved (mainly at our expense), the drugs, the gangs, the violence, problems with licences, problems with police, bankruptcy. Oh my god, the misery list for me just went on and bloody on!

A lot of people went to the club – an estimated two million over the time it was open – and I know most enjoyed themselves immensely. But whenever I do an interview that is not what my mind focuses on. I have had to rethink all that now. This book has completely changed my train of thought. It has brought to my attention all the great things that we achieved by letting Rob and Tony spend our money, because they had a vision.

I have had the pleasure of watching this book grow organically from the most important thing in our world, the people who were involved at the grass roots level. Those who worked in the club and ran it every day, who put in their hearts and souls and along the way turned it into something very special. They were hugely influential and ultimately hugely inspiring to the only people that mattered, our clubbers. The ones who paid over their hard-earned money every night for diversion, love and hope. A wonderful rapport, that I was blissfully unaware of, formed with the customers every night and became a rare brand of mutual respect, of us all being in this wonderful thing called life, together, in this strangest of cathedrals. God is a club owner.

Lifelong friendships formed over a drink and a sharing of mutual interests. A love for new music, new fashions and new friends and experiences. Memories that will last forever. Tony and Rob really didn't know what they'd begun.

It has been humbling hearing how the club and Factory Records, and the groups involved, laid a pattern for life that many people still hold dear. A message of being yourself, believing in yourself and doing what you want, when you want to. Regardless of what people say, or of what your parents thought. The thing that punk taught me was that if other punks could do it then so could I, I just had to try. That DIY ethic was at the heart of everything the Haçienda stood for: freedom, total freedom. A real 'suck-it-and-see and worry about the future later' mentality. Living in the now, for the now and sharing it with people that mattered.

I now know a lot about the people who were inspired by the Haçienda and the friends they met there, and about the wonderful things they have gone on to do in later life. Even more have gone on to be true to themselves and still relish those wonderful moments they had in the club, years later.

Musically, it's easy to list the inspired. The Chemical Brothers, Laurent Garnier, M People, Mike Pickering, Graeme Park, 808 State, through to Oasis, Primal Scream, Happy Mondays, the Stone Roses, Inspiral Carpets… The list is almost endless. And the DJs, from Hewan Clarke onwards, so many. There are other strands of culture that have benefited from the Haçienda's misfits, too. Photographers who have gone on to be very important in many areas of art: Jon Shard, Kevin Cummins, Peter Walsh, Louise Rhodes, Dave Swindells.

From a fashion point of view it's been incredible to hear how this inspiration led someone to become a Principal at Central Saint Martin College, Hywell Davies, and Head Designer at Max Mara for over three decades, thank you Ian Griffiths. Also Wayne Hemingway, Murray and Vern, Pam Hogg, Vivienne Westwood, John Richmond and many others.

I've learned of the influence the many great nights – Hot, Zumbar, Nude, Wide, Freak, Temperance and Flesh – and what they achieved in shaping people's lives and giving them freedom, not only personally but culturally too. I am a born-again Haçienda lover, only now realising how much I took for granted on the many nights I was there, worrying about all the wrong things, missing what was right in front of my nose, no pun intended. I know that drugs were a part of the culture but it turns out to be only a small part, much smaller than I thought. Most of these people were high on life. You'll see how they changed the world in this book, and did so without anything but their own iron will, hard work and a few crazy ideas. Making this mad world we all live in so much better.

I am so delighted that we didn't take Bernard Manning's advice on the opening night: "You fucking idiots should quit while you're ahead!"

Love, Hooky.

Peter Hook

Introduction

Without doubt, the Haçienda is Manchester's greatest cultural touchstone. An ever-evolving melting pot of music and fashion, this iconic nightclub is up there with the greats. It's a venue that literally changed lives.

11–13 Whitworth St East, a former yacht showroom on the wrong side of town, transcends being a mere building. For 15 years it gifted the city's clubbing fraternity with a unique space to call their own, bestowing revellers with a blueprint of idealism that still resonates to this day.

The club had delusions of grandeur, artfully conceived by Factory Records and designed to be the "anti-disco". Odd, unique and years ahead of its time, its utilitarian-chic – a bona-fide design classic – became the backdrop to 15 years of era-defining moments.

"You went through the doors and you were in this beautiful, floodlit space," remembers former general manager Ang Matthews. "It was so bright when it was first opened, a real pop of modernity. That international orange, the trademark colour of architect Ben Kelly, offsetting those pigeon-blue walls. It was the most beautiful building I've ever walked into."

"The audacity of the space took your breath away," remembers photographer Elaine Constantine. "The city wasn't prepared for such a bold statement. What had we done to deserve this?"

When the club opened its doors, in May 1982, Manchester was not the thriving metropolitan hub it would later become. Needless to say, it was the sheer chutzpah of the place – the concept, scale and magnetic attraction – which enabled this once-industrial city (the world's first, as Tony Wilson would often remind us) to reinvent itself as a dominant force.

"Growing up in Manchester in the early '80s, going to pubs and clubs was different," says longtime employee Leroy Richardson. "You normally had to dress smart, in a shirt and tie, but in the Haçienda it didn't matter what you looked like. The doormen still wore dickie bows back then, but they were also dead polite and nice. In other places we were told that having an Afro was a fire hazard. It wasn't a personal racist thing by the bouncers, it was what the owners of those clubs dictated. And then some girl would walk past with a curly perm."

"It was a place where the bouncers didn't care whether you wore smart shoes," agrees Graeme Park, later to become one of the venue's key DJs. "Up until then, clubs catered for different crowds. You had soul nights and hip-hop nights – different types of audiences for different types of music. But at the Haçienda it was hairdressers next to barristers, builders dancing next to teachers, the unemployed, and even football hooligans. Nobody gave a shit. It was a real cross section of backgrounds and cultures. Just an incredible mix."

By 1982, fragments of alternative pop, proto-Goth and a fledgling indie scene brought colour and new romance to the monochrome palette of Manchester. "I found some photographs I thought I'd lost recently," says Richardson. "It's 1982, and the people in them really sum up the times. There's a few glam people, one or two Siouxsie lookalikes, but loads of ordinary folk that probably worked in offices. Everyone looks so young."

From legendary gigs to shapeshifting club nights, the Haçienda was a cathedral of youth culture, populated by thrill-seeking

disciples from all walks of life. For those who worshipped at its altar – the bin men, the pop stars, the working-class kids and queer hedonists – it was a place to see and be seen, a Utopian democracy where race, religion and sexuality were deemed irrelevant. At the Haçienda, people came together. They sang from the same hymnbook and danced 'til they dropped. The club may have gone but its legacy remains undiminished.

"What makes Manchester different?" muses journalist and Wythenshawe boy, Paul Flynn. "I think it's a kind of Northern diffidence. It's pissing down outside, there's nothing to do and we're bored, so let's go somewhere and have the opposite of that. With the Haçienda you were presented with this kind of art-directed space, a fairly blank canvas onto which you could project ideas about yourself. And it's all done under this umbrella of good taste. I think the city was gifted good taste."

Taste aside, in many ways the Haçienda was a pure fluke, a scatterbrain idea mapped out on the back of a cigarette packet. New Order manager Rob Gretton wanted somewhere to socialise. Tony Wilson: newsman, TV face and Factory label boss, saw it as his gift to the city. There's a perceived notion that Manchester is a place that doesn't take itself too seriously. Wilson took it very seriously. Surveying the newly constructed Haçienda, he declared: "Buildings create synergy. They concentrate creativity. When the Victorians built railway stations, they didn't just put up platforms and a Portakabin. Buildings change the way people think. That's how it worked in Renaissance Florence."

"I did fall hook, line and sinker for Tony Wilson's endless publicising for the city," says Flynn. "I think what's really crucial and key to the Haçienda for me is that you weren't buying into a nightclub, it wasn't just a night out. Not that you would've processed it at the time. But when you think about it afterwards, you were buying into a whole ethos, weren't you?"

In some ways, that ethos was anarchy – not the power-dissolving blow the Sex Pistols had advocated, but the rise of individualism and Factory's inherent quest and encouragement for disorder. In many ways, this would be the club's eventual undoing, but for a few golden years there would be cash from chaos, even if it was often unequally distributed.

"Tony said he hired me because he'd seen the anarchist in me," says Ang Matthews, "but you know how Tony talked. I remember standing in the DJ box with him at the height of the club's success, and he'd say, 'look what you've done', when everyone's hands were in the air. There was always a sense you could do anything in that place, for better or for worse. There's never been anywhere like it since."

"I love that approach," says Paul Flynn. "You know? We're going to put a picture of Anthony Blunt over there, and there's going to be a Japanese lager for sale here, and we'll construct industrial bollards because we believe in JG Ballard, or whatever it is. The philosophy behind it was beautifully skewed, but it didn't matter. It didn't matter if you knew about those things or bought into it either, that wasn't important. All those things were kind of anti-fun. It was austere and brutal, and we shall not see its like again."

It's important to eschew the media myth that the Haçienda was all about drugs, guns and calamitous business decisions. Beyond the clichés, the club possessed northern soul, and it is this quality – the buzzing crowds decked out in their finest, the gritty, passionate desire to escape and partake, which should rightly take centre stage.

The club finally closed its doors in 1997, but this is a light that will never go out.

Coca-Cola

1982-

-1984

The year is 1982. Britain is bracing itself for war with Argentina, Michael Jackson releases *Thriller*, and the decade is tuning into endless modern possibilities. Within the highs and lows of these cultural shifts – the uneven politics, the optimism of shiny new pop music – the country struggles to find its feet. Trade Unions are pulling rank, unemployment soars; but where there was mud now lies glitter. Do you march or dance? Or merely march onto the dancefloor?

Meanwhile, over in Manchester, a nightclub is about to open its doors that will change the city forever. A cause célèbre of the emphatically cool Factory Records, the newly minted Haçienda is the brainchild of New Order manager Rob Gretton. On early American tours, he and the band had frequented and played at the edgiest nightclubs of New York – a clutch of genre-busting venues, which lit a metaphorical fuse. For entrepreneurial Gretton, a reluctant DJ with sizable ambitions, this was a eureka moment.

They liked what they saw: the gritty electronic music, cultivated atmosphere and the no-dress-code policy so alien to the UK. People cite the divine culture clash of Larry Levan's Paradise Garage as being a formative influence on the Haçienda, but lesser-known joints such as Tier 3 and Hurrah provided the truest inspiration. Perhaps most significantly, the epoch-defining fusion of style and sound that was Danceteria, the hippest of them all, ignited the ultimate flame. Factory boss Tony Wilson, in thrall to Manhattan's late-night agenda, followed the band to these places and duly took note. A seed was sown. Manchester deserved, nay demanded, the same if not better. "The Haçienda must be built."

Clearly inspired, debatably deluded, the Haçienda was subsequently built on Joy Division money. The aftermath of the tragic death of Ian Curtis in 1980 had the side-effect of significantly swelling the company's coffers, and so began a project (some might call it a money pit) riotously ambitious in scale and radical of design. 11–13 Whitworth Street East, a former yacht showroom located on the Rochdale Canal, was essentially just a cavernous warehouse. In the hands of designer Ben Kelly ("I thought the Haçienda sounded like an awful Mexican adobe") this lofty space – all vertiginous ceilings and countless cubic feet of fresh air – took unusual shape.

Tony Wilson, an ardent fan of his home town – "the world's first industrial city" – led the charge to inject a sizable dose of post-industrial glamour into Manchester's down-at-heel streets. Kelly gave him stark autobahn chic, applying the graphic look of Peter Saville's "Achtung!" yellow and black stripes, and an urban décor – concrete parking bollards, cat's eyes and a muted Bauhaus colour palette – last seen on the M62. "I wanted what New York had," said Wilson. "A place for the kids."

What the kids wanted was a different proposition altogether. With a crowd mostly gleaned from nearby universities, plus a generous sprinkle of local hairdressers and shop assistants, the place opened to mixed reviews from a generation more interested in cheap beer than Big Apple cool.

Journalist Alyson Walsh, then studying fashion design at Manchester Polytechnic, was one of the first through the door. "It felt like a special place, no doubt about that. New York had Studio 54, and we had the Haçienda. Of course, the Haç didn't have the high-gloss glamour, but it was a grungy northern take on it for the city's cool people. I couldn't get enough. Those huge, plastic, industrial abattoir curtains, like a hospital or something, that led you in. Then quite a long walk to the bar. When it was empty – which it often was – you felt quite self-conscious."

In these early days, the Haçienda was often short on numbers. In a venue as large as it was, even a few hundred people felt like peas rattling around in a biscuit tin. "Sometimes it would be freezing cold as well, plus the acoustics weren't great," Alyson remembers. "Which makes me wonder what the attraction was. Why did it work? I remember ordering at the bar once, and Hooky from New

01

Order was standing next to us. It felt like the coolest place ever. I mean, you were mixing with Manchester royalty."

Regal or not, early '80s Manchester, with notable exceptions, was definitely short on sartorial flair. Post-punk, although not a term used at the time, came to describe the affordable uniform so beloved of this blank generation. The dour black-and-white imagery of city heroes Joy Division, blanketed from the cold in army greatcoats, cultivated a look that defines the period. "It was all about second-hand clothes," says Walsh. "I used to wear dead men's jackets from charity shops, stuff from Affiecks Palace, and those obligatory demob overcoats. We'd make stuff at college, too, running up jersey tube skirts on the overlocker, but very shoddily. Every day was a bad hair day. I'd cut mine myself, crimp it to death, then back-comb and hairspray it to oblivion. There's probably a hole in the ozone layer over Hulme to this day."

For those less follically DIY, the Haçienda instigated its own independent hairdressers, Swing, housed directly below the stage in a basement salon that would also serve as dressing room for visiting acts. Swing was the epitome of cool in a city where hairdressers were often sharper than their scissors, and cutting edge in extreme. Run by local club promoter Andrew Berry, who would later DJ at the club, the place became the unofficial daytime HQ of Manchester's confident new swathe of bands. "I remember washing Mark E. Smith's hair one time," remembers salon junior and Factory acolyte Tracey Donnelly, "which is not something you'd forget. We had New Order in all the time, obviously, and A Certain Ratio. Andrew knew Johnny Marr too, so The Smiths would often drop in for a trim."

"I was massively into Factory Records," says Berry. "I cut Tony Wilson's hair once and begged him to give the salon its own FAC number. We ended up being FAC 98. I think I'm prouder of that than almost anything else."

While DJ Hewan Clarke gamely played the edgier floor-fillers of the period, the club relied heavily on alternative ideas. The Haçienda's formative years were unintentionally less about clubbing and more about the live experience, often booking bands passing through on northern tours. In 1982, on any given night you could catch acts as disparate as The Smiths (who played here twice) synth-wobbly Blancmange, or the Nick Cave-fronted The Birthday Party, whipping up an Antipodean storm.

"Whoever was booking those bands knew what they were doing," says Andy Polaris, former lead singer with London club band Animal Nightlife, who played at the Haçienda twice in 1983. "Most of those acts went on to have chart hits in the next few months after that."

Animal Nightlife were darlings of London's burgeoning style magazine culture, hyped and snapped to great effect. "We'd been in *The Face* magazine – a whole page – and I think that's how we got so many gigs up north. I can remember going to the Russell Club in Hulme, to follow Siouxsie and the Banshees in 1978, so I kind of knew Manchester from those days. But to walk into the Haçienda five years later was a revelation. There were very few custom-built clubs operating at that time. Most places that you played were old, run-down cabaret-type clubs, or places that had seen the best of their years. The Haçienda was sparkling new. I distinctly remember the design – all that black and yellow, like a construction site, and bollards everywhere, which I thought was a bit of a weird design element. The stage wasn't very big so the audience were right in your face, but it was a neat place to play."

As a nine-piece outfit, the stage, a small, raised rectangle, crowned with theatre lighting, did present difficulties. "We were really influenced by Kid Creole and the Coconuts, so it was a bit much with all our percussion, congas and backing singers. It felt like being on a postage stamp. But everything about the Haçienda, that whole period of history, felt very new, very fresh, and definitely different."

This first chapter proved to be a real page turner.

NO SERVICE HERE

Left // The Haçienda by day, with light streaming through the club's glass ceiling. **Kevin Cummins:** "The Haçienda looked good with the lights on – nowhere else did."

Above and opposite // From pop to punk and beyond. **Mike Pickering**: "The Haçienda was a great space to play with, the idea being that it was a cathedral of youth culture. I'd have people like William Burroughs playing on Sunday lunchtime, reading poetry, and then someone like John Cale. Everything went from one extreme to another."

Above and opposite // Good times in the early years of the club. Above is a photograph from club-goer Ann Dinan. Opposite shows Jeff Richards and then-partner Caroline in The Gay Traitor bar.

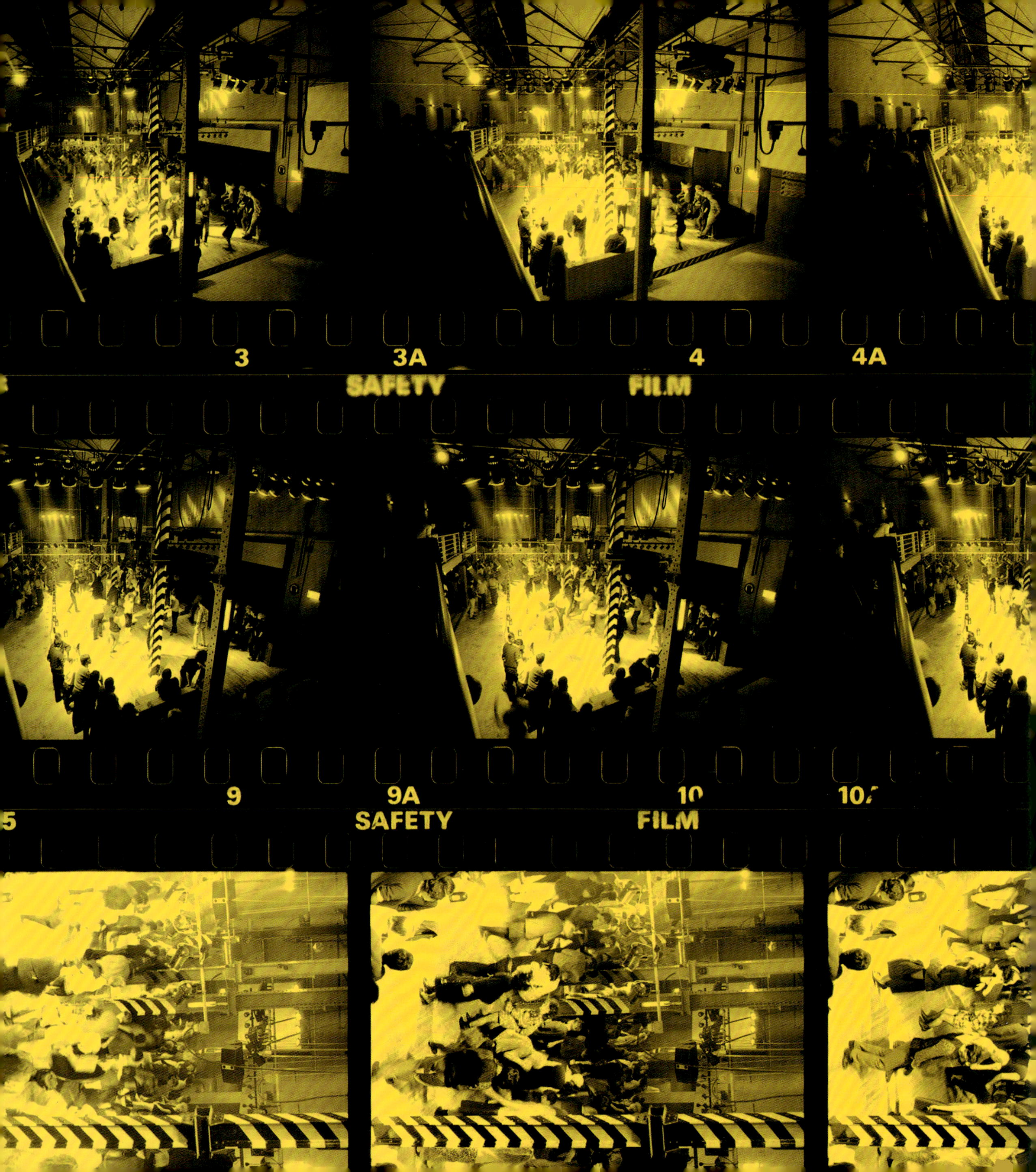
3
3A
4
4A
SAFETY
FILM
9
9A
10
SAFETY
FILM

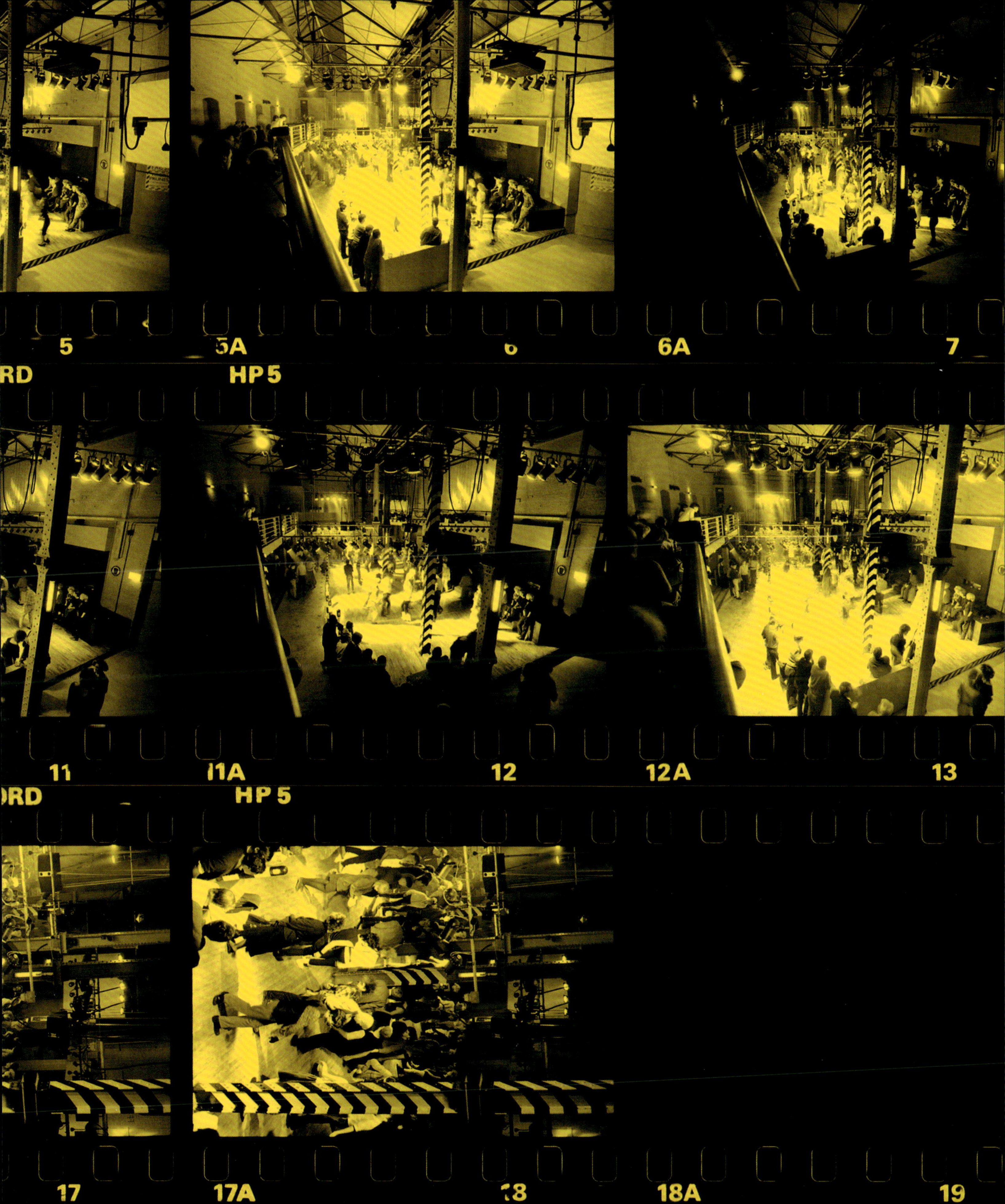
5
5A
6
6A
7
RD
HP 5
11
11A
12
12A
13
ORD
HP 5
17
17A
18
18A
19

THIS CLOAKROOM
WILL NOT ACCEPT
REAL FUR
ALL ITEMS NOT CLAIMED
AFTER 21 DAYS
WILL BE DISPOSED OF
AVOID THE CLOAKROOM
QUEUE - COLLECT YOUR
COAT EARLY
50 PENCE PER ITEM
MAXIMUM CAPACITY 1400
NO ADMITTANCE

SOLD OUT
GUEST LIST ONLY
NO SERVICE
AT THIS END OF THE BAR
NO ALCOHOL
SERVED
AFTER 2a.m.

EIGHT MANCHESTER DESIGNERS
FAC 51
The Hacienda + Vidal Sassoon
present
Thursday 6th December 1984
10·30pm onwards
"STYLE IN OUR TIME"
Hair/Fashion Event
SPECIAL GUESTS
The Jazz Defektors
(DANCE)
and
Frankies Angels
Admission: £2.50
& £2.00 concession.
Tickets available from HMV, Paperchase, Piccadilly Records, The Hacienda and Vidal Sassoon.
Design: Anagram Studios 061 833 9299
11/13 WHITWORTH ST. WEST. MANCHESTER. TEL: 061-236 5051

Left and above // Style In Our Time was a fashion extravaganza put together by the Haçienda's then-manager, Ellie Gray, showcasing young, up-and-coming designers with a catwalk show populated by models and dancers including Frankies Angels (above). **Alison Knight** (who took these photographs) remembered: "Everything seemed possible then."

Above // The early 1980s sketchbook of Manchester fashion designer **John Richmond**, "inspired by nights at the Haçienda, with a classic art school coloured-in photo booth portrait – we had to do filters by hand back in the day".

Mani is a musician and was a member of the club.

This was taken on my first night at the Haçienda. I was wearing my WW2 flying jacket and probably some Levi's 501s, a shirt and a pair of adidas Samba.

My best night at the club would have to be playing there with the Stone Roses. Having been a member since it first opened I'd seen so many bands there, so it felt like something of an achievement to walk the stage where I'd watched New Order and the Bunnymen – bands who I adored.

Mani

In Conversation

Ang Matthews is a former manager of the Haçienda.

Graham Massey is founding member of electronic music group 808 State, formative members of the acid house scene.

Suddi Raval is a DJ and electronic dance music pioneer. He was a Haçienda regular and one half of the group Together.

Peter J Walsh is a photographer who captured images of many nights at the club.

Graham: I always think of the Haçienda as a page-turning episode in the city because Manchester was completely changed by that place. It was the first inkling of any sophistication in the nightlife scene.

Before, it was just working men's clubs and there was a particular attitude to going out; it was almost like a mating ritual where men and women were in defined roles. What it represented to me was a new world view in a tiny, claustrophobic city.

Suddi: I think it is one of the most important things to ever happen in popular culture. What happened there had such a profound effect on pretty much everything to this day. No way in the world did I expect that we'd still be talking about it now. We knew back then that what was happening was important, new and different and that something was possibly going to change, but the extent of it is just unbelievable.

Everything shook up and everyone saw the world in a completely different way after going. I came out a different person, I was a fashion student at Ashton College, but I have had a career in music and sound because of what I experienced at the Haçienda.

Peter: I remember going to clubs like Rotters and The Ritz and they were laid with bad, beer-soaked carpets and there were fights constantly. Now there was no dress code. You could turn up in jeans and trainers and just walk in. At the beginning it was this huge, fairly empty space with incredible design, music, art and fashion. I think it transformed everybody's lives. When you went there, especially during the acid house period, it was like nothing you'd ever seen before.

Ang: Everywhere else was much smaller. Although it wasn't a big club, the licence was only for 1,200, but I used to squeeze in 1,900 and you couldn't move after that. Nowadays everything is 5,000 and over, which I think is too big to get that feel. For us it was the right space at the right time.

Graham: It had a family feel to it, which is quite unique of a club. You weren't always on the dancefloor, a lot of the time you were hanging out in corners or on the balcony – it was like a whole department store of nightclubbing.

Ang: Before, I can't think of anywhere I would have gone as a woman on my own. You could walk into the Haçienda and even if none of your mates were there, you could sit with the bar staff – it had a real community feel. You didn't have to dress up or put on makeup, you instantly felt comfortable.

Peter: You'd go in and see people like Bernard from New Order, or A Guy Called Gerald and Inspiral Carpets, and everyone would be chatting and sharing ideas or asking what people were up to. There was a real sense of community with the artists, too. It was a melting pot of creativity.

Graham: I always viewed it as a gig venue. I remember Mantronix playing there as a really important night. It was the first time I'd seen the club full, and it took the temperature of a new youth movement in Manchester because the audience was a lot younger at that point.

The late '80s was important for acid house. Mike Pickering would play on a Friday, and he might only play an hour of that music, but it was a real eclectic mix. It was geared towards dancers and people would give them a respected space to dance. The music was there to serve them.

Suddi: My introduction was when I was 16. That's also when house music was starting to get big. Even though I was 16, I looked about 12 and I had to sneak in with people because I'd been to clubs before where the door staff had asked me where my mum was! The queue used to be so big that we would go down at about 7 o'clock in the evening and people would be giving out free copies of the *Freaky Dancing* zine to people who were waiting.

I was really nervous to go. My dad was quite strict, but the first time that I went I was instantly addicted. I literally went every single night that I could after that. It was unbelievable to witness the energy in there. It was something that the whole world was watching as there was so much press coverage.

Peter: People were coming from all over the country and from across Europe as well. I was working for the *NME* at the time, and they'd send me down to photograph what was going on, but I also used to go down on my own because I began to realise that it was a really significant moment culturally.

I think a big part of the attraction was the space itself. It was purpose built for the acid house scene, although they didn't realise it.

Ang: Very few people were looking at the DJ, which is very different to what it's like now. They were once at the side of the stage and the punters couldn't see them at all.

Graham: When you first heard your music being played there, that was a breakthrough. It felt so special to deliver to the club in such a full circle. When nights like Hot began, we'd leave the studio with a cassette of music that we'd made specifically for the Haçienda. Jon Dasilva would then play the cassette and we'd go back to the studio to tweak it after hearing it through the sound system.

Suddi: The music that I was writing was completely designed around my experiences there. I was writing tunes before I went in and it's almost like when I stepped foot in the club, it told me how to arrange the music I was making. We hoped we'd hear it played in there, it was our dream.

When it did get played, we had said to Mike Pickering, "We've got this record, we've just pressed it. Would you have a listen?" Jonathan [Donaghy] knew quite a few people so we managed to get into the DJ booth and when we heard 'Hardcore Uproar' getting mixed in it completely blew our minds. We couldn't believe it.

Graham: It says something about a place that the DJ would have an interaction with a local musician like that. The community atmosphere in the club meant that you could have a conversation with the people who were programming the music. There was such a social mix, there was doctors, nurses, binmen and postmen partying together and there were no borders between anyone. It felt so fresh and different from anything before.

There was a general sense of socialism in Manchester where no one could get too big for their boots. It was considered very uncool to put a hierarchy on things.

Peter: I was photographing everyone in the space. Not only the ravers, but the people who were working there as well, because they were also partying after their shift. The whole thing was so interesting, it was like its own lifeform – everything was intertwined.

Graham: You were going to get sweaty, so you had to wear as little as possible really. There's a photo of me on the dancefloor wearing a puffer jacket and my Filofax with a strap one night, which probably wasn't my greatest idea. Other than that, we'd wear a lot of long-sleeved t-shirts.

Ang: I used to wear a lot of cycling shorts and tight trousers with stirrups and big white high-top trainers. It used to be so hot in there and I didn't have a lot of clothes in those days, so I'd wear a lot of the free band t-shirts too.

Suddi: I used to make these big baggy tops as I was a fashion student at the time, and I made one with a huge, dilated pupil on the back that everyone would want to know where it was from. I had a plan to sell them and make millions, but that never happened.

Ang: I saw a girl wearing a strap-on dildo and gaffa tape on her nipples at a Flesh night.

Suddi: I grew up in a really tough town where nearly everyone was out of work and racism was a really big thing. It was normal for me to keep my head down. Fighting was a normal thing, there was nothing else to do. I was so used to racism, it was just a part of life. When I went there, it was obvious before spending a long time there that I'd never ever felt remotely safe anywhere before, but in there I felt unbelievably safe and incredibly comfortable. I could go on my own and meet people, and that was so refreshing.

I know for a fact that there were people that had aggressive demeanours before they went and the space completely changed their outlook. People were completely open to things that they would not have been as comfortable with before.

Ang: It taught me that you can have a job that's just so fun. It was the first time that I had been in a position where men actually listened to what I had to say, and I could tell that they valued my opinion.

Opposite // Later to become manager of the Haçienda, Ang Matthews was photographed here by Peter J Walsh for *The Face*.

"Everything about the club looked anti-fun – very austere and brutal. It was great that they had the idea of throwing what was Mancunian at that canvas. It was constantly copied after that. Everything related back to the Haçienda. Even now, when you go around Manchester, everything relates back to that time."

Ang Matthews

Previous // A DJ mixes on stage during a Kurtis Blow concert on January 24, 1983.

Above and opposite // Nick Cave and The Birthday Party, photographed at the club in February 1983 (above) and performing there the previous year (opposite).

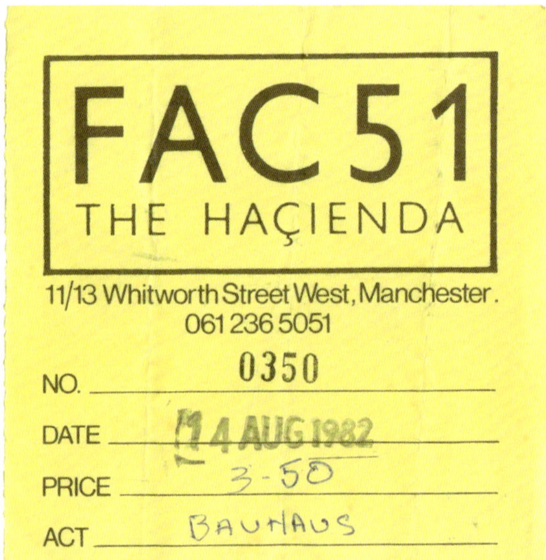

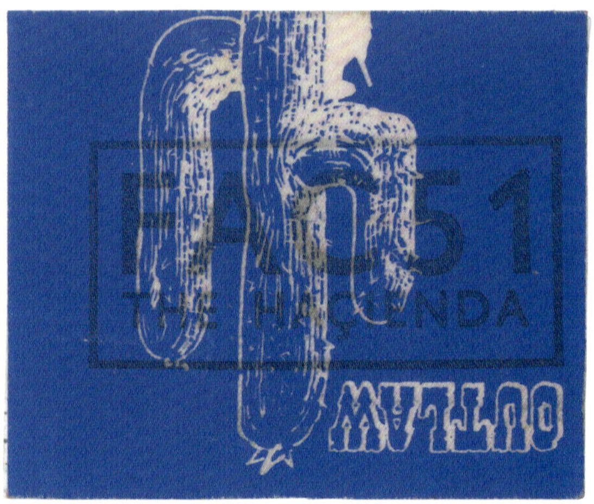

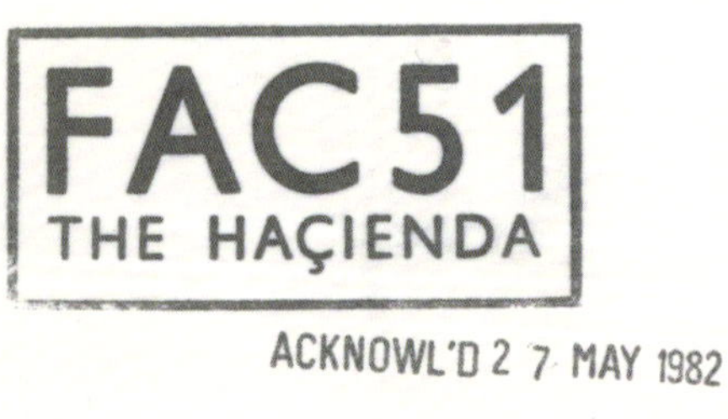

Left // Early mementoes from the club, including a security badge crudely fashioned out of a membership form (top) and a ticket from the club's opening week (bottom).

Opposite // Graham Massey: "It had a family feel to it, which is quite unique of a club. You weren't always on the dancefloor, a lot of the time you were hanging out in corners or on the balcony – it was like a whole department store of nightclubbing."

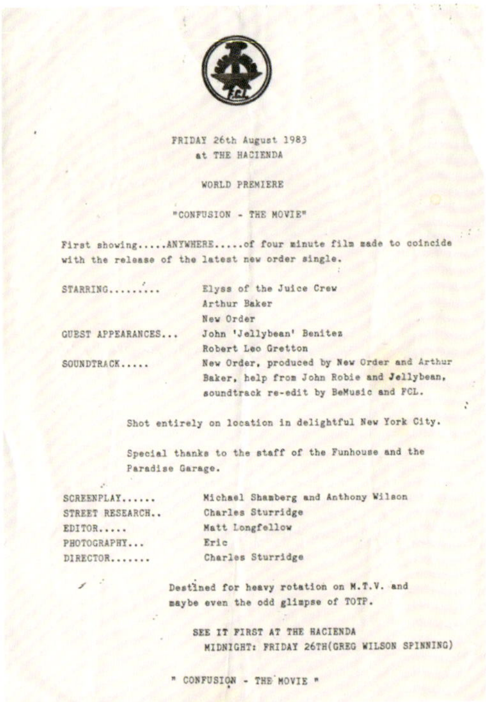

FRIDAY 26th August 1983
at THE HACIENDA

WORLD PREMIERE

"CONFUSION - THE MOVIE"

First showing.....ANYWHERE.....of four minute film made to coincide with the release of the latest new order single.

STARRING......... Elyss of the Juice Crew
Arthur Baker
New Order

GUEST APPEARANCES... John 'Jellybean' Benitez
Robert Leo Gretton

SOUNDTRACK..... New Order, produced by New Order and Arthur Baker, help from John Robie and Jellybean, soundtrack re-edit by BeMusic and FCL.

Shot entirely on location in delightful New York City.

Special thanks to the staff of the Funhouse and the Paradise Garage.

SCREENPLAY...... Michael Shamberg and Anthony Wilson
STREET RESEARCH.. Charles Sturridge
EDITOR..... Matt Longfellow
PHOTOGRAPHY... Eric
DIRECTOR....... Charles Sturridge

Destined for heavy rotation on M.T.V. and maybe even the odd glimpse of TOTP.

SEE IT FIRST AT THE HACIENDA
MIDNIGHT: FRIDAY 26TH(GREG WILSON SPINNING)

" CONFUSION - THE MOVIE "

Top // As co-owners of the club, New Order were inevitable regular performers, also screening a world premier of a short film to accompany the single 'Confusion' at the club.

Bottom and opposite // Edinburgh's Hey Elastica! played at the club, part of a steady stream of performers in its gig-focused early years

FAC 51
THE HAÇIENDA
Thursday 2nd June
BATCAVE
Thursday 9th June
HEY ELASTICA!
Thursday 16th June
FUNBOY THREE
Friday 17th June
HUNTERS
& COLLECTORS
Wednesday 22nd June
CURTIS MAYFIELD
Thursday 23rd June
SET THE TONE
N.B. Bands On Stage 10.00p.m.
11-13 WHITWORTH ST., WEST, MANCHESTER
061-236 5051

And a big "MUCHAS GRACIAS" to all this lot for appearing in 1983 . . . .

NEW ORDER
QUANDO QUANGO
DURUTTI COLUMN
A CERTAIN RATIO
52nd STREET
SECTION 25
JAMES
STOCKHOLM MONSTERS
THE ROYAL FAMILY & THE POOR
LAVOLTA LAKOTA
THE FALL
VIOLENT FEMMES
GRANDMASTER FLASH
KLAUS SCHULZE
ORANGE JUICE
CLOCK D.V.A.
D. NOTES
LITTLE STEVEN & HIS DISCIPLES
VISCIOUS PINK PHENOMENA
THE BOX
PRINCE CHARLES
SECRET 7
C.P. LEE & CO FOR NEWGATE
ROBERT PALMER
THE BAT CAVE TOUR
SHREIKBACK
HEY ELASTICA
THOMPSON TWINS
FUN BOY 3
HUNTERS & COLLECTORS
KURTIS BLOW
CURTIS MAYFIELD
MATT FRETTON
THE SMITHS
CENTRAL LINE
DEFUNCT
THE ALARM
HOWARD DEVOTO
JAH WOBBLE
ONE THE JUGGLER
ANIMAL NIGHTLIFE
ROMAN HOLIDAY
AUBREYHAHA
LYDIA LUNCH
KING
NEUTRAMENT
O.M.D.
BRILLIANT
THE RESPOND PACKAGE
JOHN FOXX
THE JAZZ DEFECTORS

ALAN VEGA
FAD GADGET
THE DANCING TARANTULAS
PAUL HAIG
JO BOXERS
TEST DEPARTMENT
SHEER IMAGE
DANSE SOCIETY
S.P.K.
ICICLE WORKS
DIVINE
VIRGIN PRUNES
CHINA CRISIS
CAMELEONS
THOMAS DOLBY
EURYTHMICS
PALE FOUNTAINS
JOHN CALE
SISTERS OF MERCY
BEAST
EDDIE & SUNSHINE
PIG BAG
THE UNDERTONES
DISCOBOLISC
SET THE TONE
CABARET VOLTAIRE
FOREIGN PRESS
BIRTHDAY PARTY
STRAWBERRY SWITCHBLADE
WHOUDINI
LITTLE BIG BAND
LIFE
MY AMERICAN WIFE
ARMOURY SHOW
WILD HONEY
EINSTURZENDE NEUBATEN
FRANKIE GOES TO HOLLYWOOD
GARY GLITTER
NICO
THE PORCH PARTY

. . . . and for the
special appearance of . . . . .

HOWARD MARSHALL JONES

Left and opposite // The 1983 roll-call of performers, from the obscure to household names, including a March performance by the Eurythmics, captured by a club-goer and her friends (below left).

Hewan Clarke was the Haçienda's first-ever resident DJ.

The first time I went into the Haçienda I couldn't believe it. There was absolutely nothing like it in Manchester. Walking in there was like walking onto the set of *Blade Runner*, it was magnificent. It wasn't a nightclub, it was like a self-built art gallery.

I was the first DJ that worked at the club and I'd DJ with some of the bands that were on the Factory label. Practically every band that was around in the '80s that made it big played there.

The team behind it were very innovative. Tony [Wilson] had some really weird ideas, but they all worked. I was playing a lot of jazz, funk and soul, they wanted Black music, so that's what I was playing.

The club completely changed my life. Being up there in the DJ box and playing music was transformative.

The club was a very daring idea. There were other clubs that were opening around that time, but they were just typical nightclubs. Nobody had the vision that Tony Wilson and his crew had, they wanted something special. When you walked in it was amazing. You had the art, the colours, the walk-through and the curtains to the dancefloor. It was life-changing.

When The Factory – which was formally the PSV Club in Hulme – shut down, all the crowd that went there followed Tony to the new club. I got a bit of stick at first because they were used to hearing the punk records that were played at The Factory and I didn't play that stuff, but that's why the Haçienda was great, because it attracted a lot of different people from a lot of different backgrounds.

You'd have a group of people over in one corner and then another that would be scattered all over the place, but it all worked. There was another group that would always be sat downstairs in The Gay Traitor, and they'd be happy just sitting down and chatting – not everybody came to dance, a lot of people came to just be there.

I got to know bands like A Certain Ratio because they'd come to jazz clubs that I was playing in at the time. There was an integral part in history where they were about to do a tour and they asked me to go with them, so I would warm up for them before they'd come on. That's how I got to know Tony [Wilson], because he was their manager at the time.

He really liked what I was playing, which was mainly jazz, and he said to me "in a couple of years' time I want to open a club in Manchester and I want you to be the DJ", so two years before it was even a thing I knew I'd got the job. I was expecting a small club of about 200 people, I ended up with a theatre of over 1,000.

FAC51
THE HAÇIENDA

FAC51
THE HAÇIENDA

Application for membership:

NAME: [illegible]

ADDRESS: 36, old Broadway M20

DATE OF BIRTH: 20 2.50

WHAT YOU WANT FROM THE HACIENDA: My money back!

I am over 18 years of age.
I agree to be bound by the rules of the club.

SIGNATURE: [illegible]

Admission to members only

For official use only

N.

A.

D.O.B.

Nr.

D. STAMP.

FAC51	The Hacienda, 11/13 Whitworth Street West, Manchester, M3 3AL.
FUNCTION	Club, Disco, Videotek, Venue, Club.
TELEPHONE	061-236-5051.
OPENING	May 21st, 1982.
FACILITIES	3 Levels, 3 Bars, Dancefloor (136m²), Stage (72.25m²), Restaurant, Balconies, Basement.
CAPACITY	1, 650.
DANCEFLOOR SOUND	Equipment by Court, Proflex & Altec. 2.5K.
DANCEFLOOR LIGHT	Control Equipment by Gamma. 15,000 watts of lighting. 43km of 1.5mm hard wire.
VIDEO	2 × 2540mm low gain screens, 2 × Sony VPK 720PS video projection units and power packs.
COLOURS	Pigeon Blue, Poppy, RAF Blue, Aztec Gold, Salmon Red, Black, Aluminium, Pale Gold, Goose Grey, Signal Red & Light Orange.
APPROACH	Industrial Fantasy.
GENERAL MANAGER	Howard Jones.
BOOKER	Mike Pickering.
DESIGN	Ben Kelly/Peter Saville (Graphics).
LIGHTS, SOUND, VIDEO	Martin Disney.
ADMISSION	Members Only.
MEMBERSHIP	£5.25 per annum.
AGE LIMIT	Over 18.
APPLICATION	Passport photograph, SAE, and cheque made payable to FAC51 Ltd., and sent to The Hacienda, 11/13 Whitworth Street West, Manchester, M3 3AL.
INTENTION	To restore a sense of place. 'The Hacienda must be built.'

Licensing regulations attendant on the building of The Hacienda mean that admission to the club is restricted to members only. We will endeavour to keep our door and drink prices as low as possible. Membership will be £5.25 per annum. We believe that this is a small price to pay for a higher state of awareness.

'Well, you've blown it now. You'll never see The Hacienda. It doesn't exist anywhere. THE HACIENDA MUST BE BUILT.'

G21

Above // 'My money back!' The first membership form for the club. On opening, the club's licence meant that all attendees were required to be members or invited as guests – greatly affecting numbers in the early years. This form was completed by none other than Tony Wilson.

Above // This portrait of Anthony Blunt, art historian and notorious Soviet spy, hung in the Haçienda's downstairs cocktail bar, The Gay Traitor.

FAC 51
THE HAÇIENDA

THE GAY TRAITOR

In The Haçienda

Cocktail Bar opens Monday:–
5.30p.m. to 2.00a.m.

La Coçina provides the food.
The Gay Traitor the setting.

Happy ½ hour 7.30p.m. to 8.00p.m.
(aren't we cheap) on Cocktails.

The upstairs part of the Haçienda is now closed Monday nights.

Above and opposite // Gay Traitor mementoes. Regular clubber **Tommy** remembers: "I went to the Haçienda on the second week of opening and lasted through to acid house and the rave scene, along with my friends Baz and Woody. Some truly memorable times. We used to arrive early to experience two guys, Glen and Gerry, running The Gay Traitor bar in the cellar. Two truly fabulous, genuine, friendly and above all entertaining guys, like having your own private stage show."

1984-

-1986

George Orwell was right, 1984 was a special year. The great auteur's vision had predicted a tight, constrictive future, but the transition into this pivotal date felt smooth, modern and ultimately box-fresh. Synapse-popping electro music made the connection between Kraftwerk and Afrika Bambaataa, a musical wake-up call that crash-landed on the dancefloor in a riot of spinning limbs and digital hand-claps. At its roots was a streetwise sub-culture that had found its time. But the sound was broad and egalitarian, and all types of pop variants soon found their niche.

Into this arena, 25-year-old Madonna Louise Ciccone made her presence felt. Blending electronic disco, home-spun fashion and a cannelloni's worth of Italian attitude, the proto-material girl was on the precipice of a fame no one could have imagined. On 25 July 1984, as part of an outside broadcast for Tyne Tees' *The Tube*, the relatively unknown singer took to the Haçienda dancefloor – her first appearance on British TV – and lip-synched to three numbers, bouncing around the club's sprung dancefloor like an over-zealous Zumba instructor.

"I thought she was shit," spits Mike Pickering, an important figure in the club's ascendance. "The place was full, but most people stood around with their arms folded, and that characteristic Mancunian 'impress me' look on their faces. I was introduced to her as 'Mike from Quando Quango', my band from the early '80s. 'Oh, that dross,' she replied. I thought, this is going to be a long fucking day."

Head-hunted by fellow Man City fan Rob Gretton, Pickering was initially hired to book bands and mould the Haçienda's ill-defined music policy. Fittingly, he is now credited as the eyes and ears of this early period, and would later become the standout figure who would crystallise the venue's success. But his disdain for Madonna that day was not universally shared.

"I thought she was great," says Manchester-born fashion designer John Richmond. "I just happened to be there that night, but soon realised by the amount of people squashed into the club – it was heaving – that this was the shape of things to come."

"I remember it well," recalls Andrew Berry, the music-obsessed hairdresser from Swing who would simultaneously morph into one of the club's more progressive DJs. "The whole of Manchester wanted to get in on that occasion, it was such a hot ticket. The place was rammed."

Filmed in the afternoon, the club was bathed in sunshine that summer's day, the result of an inherited glass roof that would seasonally hinder the venue's ambience. "Did we realise her potential," Berry ponders. "Probably not, but people are still talking about that performance to this very day. Divisive but popular is how I would describe it."

Despite the purist ambivalence, Madonna's appearance put the Haçienda firmly on the map. She brought a certain New York cool to a new, but then decidedly uncool, Manchester. They were poles apart, but united in their dedication to the pursuit of unknown dancefloor pleasures.

For club regular Darren Harcourt, these early transitional years were an important part of forging an identity. "It's not a hip statement, but the turning point for me was seeing Jeffrey Daniel from Shalamar moonwalk on *Top of the Pops*. There was something about that asymmetric wedge haircut and his London-inspired dress sense that really appealed to me. But ultimately it was the way he moved – that early robotic body-popping you'd soon see in every shopping centre in the UK. We'd stand on the barren dancefloor of the Haçienda, jerking and ticking like teenage robots. No one is looking at you, but secretly you'd hope someone might steal a glance at your moves. At the Haçienda, I always thought I was in some kind of futurist amphitheatre, where the world is looking on, applauding my modernity."

Manchester had changed, and in a good way. Over at Spin Inn records on Cross St, the latest US 12" disco imports made the journey in town with immaculate timing. Early Haçienda DJs were finding their feet and encouraging the slowly building crowds to get on theirs. In 1985, Chad Jackson, a young hip-hop-fixated enthusiast from Wigan, entered the fray with a lust for life and an ear for a tune.

02

"For me, it was always about music. I started at the Haçienda in 1985, with a residency on Saturday night, just before the house music thing appeared and eventually took over. I've looked back at some of my playlists and I think I was the first person to actually spin a house record there. I played 'On And On' by Jesse Saunders, which is probably one of the original classics, but the one I really remember was JM Silk's 'Music Is the Key' on DJ International records. When I first went to the club, I was like, Oh man, I'd really love to play here. I guess it was just blind ambition, stuff I can't do these days because I'd feel too embarrassed. In those days I just went for things. There was always a sense that someone was willing to take a chance on you."

A major turning point for the Haçienda, and a night that came to characterise this laissez-faire attitude, was Nude. Mike Pickering was an early advocate of musical breadth, where no one genre should dominate the mix. To this end he encompassed an eclectic mix that threaded hip-hop, electro, even salsa into a seamless flow that was ultimately years ahead of its time. But DJing was never the plan. "It was a case of, well, I've tried everyone else and no one really got it. There was only Greg Wilson who understood. Everyone else wanted a microphone, and I wasn't having that, I'd been to Paradise Garage! We were one of the first clubs in the UK to just mix. We'd seen it all over America, with people like Larry Levan and Arthur Baker."

Nude was a concept, and the first named night that took off where others had faltered. "In Manchester at the time, you wouldn't get into clubs with the gear we were wearing, but they'd let in what we called 'thugs in ties', a bloke with a shirt and tie on who'd go in and beat the shit out of someone and be an absolute twat for the night. We wanted to change all that."

The Haçienda subsequently became a more democratic spot frequented by a younger, streetwise crowd. Suddenly, kids in trainers and tracksuits bowled through the doors – a sweatshirt-clad assortment of Perry boys and terrace casuals who were just as willing to dance to New Order's 'Confusion' as they were Sharon Redd. For the first time, the dancefloor was alive with people making shapes rather than joints.

On paper, the Haçienda sounds like it was at the epicentre of a burgeoning dance music revolution, but it's easy to forget that at this juncture, the club was still reliant on bands to draw in the crowds. To that end, Pickering made sure the acts he booked were as diverse as the tunes that followed. In 1984 and 1985, the breadth of choice occupying the space was a roll call of mesmerising diversity. Memorable acts included the pin-eyed ex-New York Doll, Johnny Thunders, Grandmaster Flash & the Furious Five, and the feedback frenzy of The Jesus and Mary Chain, duly bottled for their 17-minute sonic assault on the ears of a less-than-receptive audience.

It wasn't all fun and games, though. "Liz Fraser of the Cocteau Twins was upset all the way through their sound check," recalls Pickering, "the acoustics were all wrong." He was also alarmed by the sight of a gun on stage, next to reggae star Gregory Isaacs. "I thought, fucking hell, is this a sign of things to come? I wasn't far off the mark, was I?"

On a no-less-explosive note, this period was also the advent of the Haçienda's long-standing relationship with Manchester's increasingly visible gay community. The future Entertainments Manager, Paul Cons, promoted a Lesbian & Gay Miners Benefit in March 1985, and "Gay Monday" was launched to modest success that same year. Drag legend Divine shook her maracas, disco agitators The Communards acted up, and German cult romantics Gina X Performance all paved the way for a beleaguered gay youth who deserved to be noticed. The club was hitting its stride, exclusive yet inclusive at the same time. And the best was yet to come.

Left // March 27, 1985, saw A Mega Miners Benefit, hosted by Lesbians and Gays Support the Miners, featuring a performance from Pete Shelley, gay cabaret and "comedy – outrageous, witty, anarchic and crap".

Opposite // Scenes from the miners' benefit (top left, top right, bottom right) and a gig by The Cramps in 1984 (bottom left). Cramps fan **Phil** remembers: "The Haçienda had a glass roof and being a summer evening it was still very light when the doors opened, which seemed a little incongruous for a Cramps gig. The sun had gone down by the time this picture was taken though."

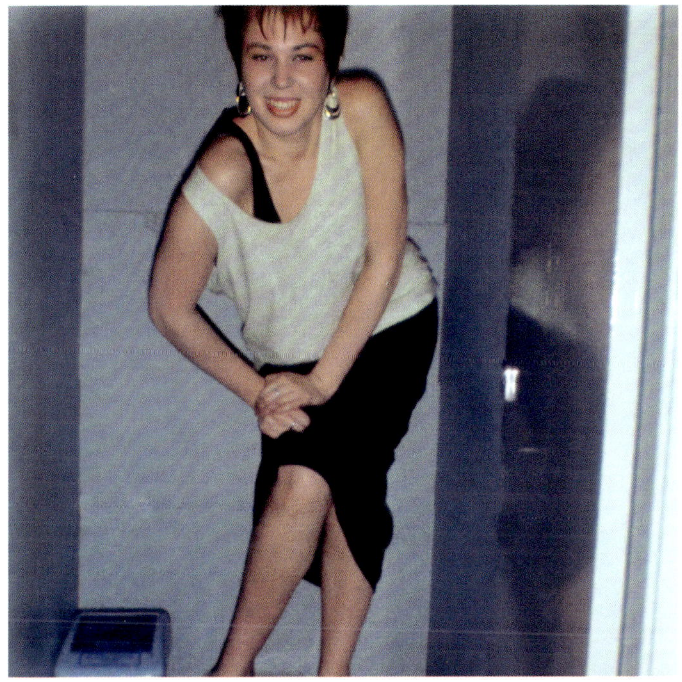

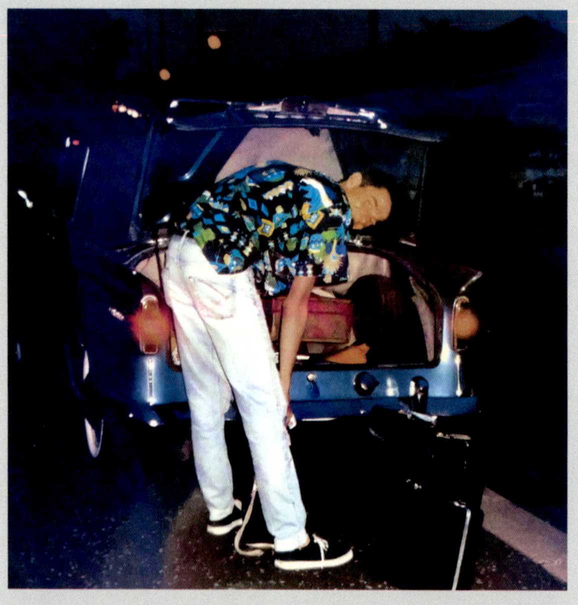

Above // Members of the extended Haçienda family: promoter and DJ John Tracy (top left, bottom left), Liz Page (top right) and Mike Pickering with Quando Quango collaborator Gonnie.

Opposite // Assorted material from the club's early years, including a DIY access-all-areas badge, and a ticket to an August 1984 concert by New York Doll and Heartbreaker, Johnny Thunders.

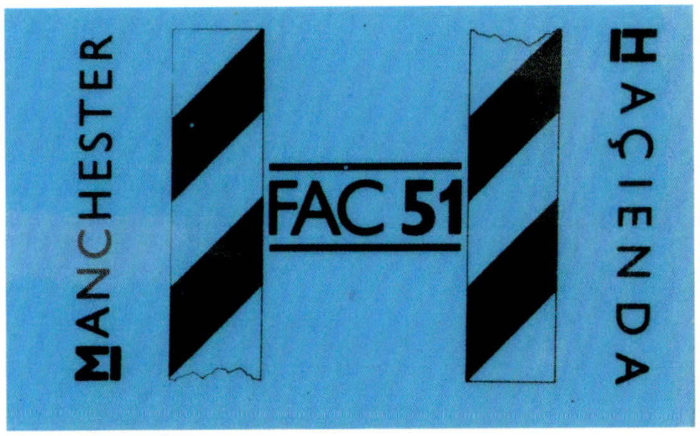
MANCHESTER
FAC 51
HAÇIENDA

FAC 51
THE HACIENDA
ALL AREAS A1

MANCHESTER
FAC 51
HAÇIENDA
JOHNNY THUNDERS
Wednesday 29th August
Tickets for all gigs available from
HMV, Paperchase, Piccadilly Records and the Hacienda.
No Membership Required
11/13 WHITWORTH ST. WEST. MANCHESTER.TEL: 061-236 5051

Ian Griffiths is a fashion designer and the Creative Director of Max Mara. He was a Haçienda regular in the early years of the club's life.

Peter Hook is a musician and co-owner of the Haçienda.

Ian: The years I spent in Manchester were the best years of my life. Living in Hulme was like a community. It was a condemned council estate that had only been built about 12 years prior to us moving in. It was Thatcher's Britain and there seemed to be no future for us, nobody was interested in what we were doing or what we liked. We were just making our own culture.

I left Manchester in 1987, so I was going to the club in its early days. In the beginning you could go there every single night, and that's what I did. There'd be a handful of people there and it was great, it used to be like being at home in your living room. You used to get a plate of chips, half a lager and have a dance.

Peter: I used to have to go to eat because I had no money. At home I wasn't eating anywhere near as well as I was when I was at the club. The chicken pancakes were fantastic.

It used to be open all day, so you used to hear some pretty wacky stuff, because the DJ would be there for hours.

Ian: You could dance to things that you would never have dared dance to previously. The difference between the Haçienda and other clubs that were around at that time was that you didn't get the feeling that it was owned by someone who was solely out to make money. You got the feeling that it was yours, for you. You were completely safe there and no one was in any way exploiting you.

Peter: Tony [Wilson] wanted it to be like a youth club. He wanted all the misfits in Manchester to be able to go somewhere where they were welcome 24 hours a day, seven days a week. It was his ambition.

Ian: Tony Wilson was like an uncle to me, he was a huge part of the community. By the time the club opened, we were morphed into a subculture that didn't really have a particular name. It wasn't post-punk, it wasn't new wave and it wasn't New Romantic or Post-Romantic, it was something else completely. It was completely our own. Everything was so fluid in those days.

For me, music and fashion are indistinguishable. Music is how fashion expressed itself and you couldn't separate them. The look went with the music, and it really was about trying to keep up and ahead.

I started making clothes because I just couldn't resist. I was supposed to be studying architecture, but I was messing around on my friend's sewing machine and buying these golden fabrics from Rusholme and making pairs of elasticated trousers that got more and more extravagant.

My time at the club totally informed where I'm coming from in my fashion career. Whenever you went out back then, everything was about image. You did it for the people who were present, you played out your life for the people who were around you and who were there.

We went through phases. There was the rag stage, which was around the time of 'Buffalo Gals', and we'd wear layers and layers of torn dirty clothes that would totally contrast with our perfect makeup. I also remember wearing a blue leather suit that I had made – it was very Kraftwerk. We would debut all kinds of different looks and we felt safe to do so.

I would not be working in fashion now if it wasn't for the Haçienda. I would not have found my way into fashion, and I would not have had the viewpoint that I have. The thing that has made me successful as a designer is that I've always brought a little bit of edginess into what we do. I've learned to play with quite a classic conservative aesthetic, whilst making it a little bit radical at the same time.

Peter: You felt safe in your circle there. The club gave you that security and freedom because before that there was nowhere else in Manchester that would.

Ian: Walking in there was like walking into a cathedral. It was so high and big, and I thought everything sounded amazing and important. Everything was reverberating just like it would do in a cathedral.

The dancefloor was incredible, it was so good to dance on because it was so big and sprung and very often you'd be the only people dancing.

It was the most influential period of my life, without a doubt. Those few years in Manchester formed the basis of everything I've done since.

Previous page and this page // Ian Griffiths photographed by Kevin Cummins.

ILFORD
18
17

The whole of Manchester wanted to get in on that occasion, it was such a hot ticket. The place was rammed… Divisive but popular is how I would describe it.

Andrew Berry

MC Tunes is a DJ and musician.

I was about 15 when the Haçienda first opened, and it was originally a club for alternative music and that was my experience. By the time it got to the house music scene, I was on tour with 808 State doing my thing. But before it got to that stage, I remember it being a mecca for funk, punk and R&B music.

I'm from Moss Side, so when Manchester's indie scene was really big and you had all sorts of bands signing to Factory, I was making hip-hop tracks with the likes of Rap Assassins and A Guy Called Gerald. Going to the club when the bands were playing in the early days was a bit of an alternative night for me, it almost felt posh, as it was a completely different vibe to what I was used to in Moss Side.

I was more influenced by the bands that were attached than the later club scene. Like when I heard the remix of 'Hallelujah' and huge electronic tracks like New Order's 'Blue Monday' – we used to breakdance to that shit!

The remixes started happening and they began to bridge the big gap. I was brought up on hip-hop and black music, bands like Parliament and Earth, Wind & Fire, so when it started to crossover with the remixes, that was really impressive. That's when we all thought "fuck, that's it, the Haçienda is going off".

It never would have worked without Tony Wilson. He was a true media icon, and when he was doing *Granada Reports* nobody really knew what he was doing. He bought a club called the PSV Club in Hulme, right next to where I grew up. When Tony passed away, the club had already shut down. Peter [Hook] and Tony were true believers, and you need that. I'm just glad that they both understood the value of the brand and kept it alive, because the vibe is bigger than the club and it incorporates all the incredible Black music that I was raised on.

When I first went there everybody was dressed very sharply. There were a lot of different styles, not the tube tops and glowsticks that it's now renowned for. It was more punk-rock, funky, totally different to anywhere that I'd been before. It was a huge gathering of individuality in a place that people could call home. Personally, my style at the time was centred on baggy pants, big trainers like Nike Airs and a hoodie. And you could get into the club like that when it first opened.

I think it's the idea and the memory of what it stands for, which is "let's just forget about all of that and just party". I've always been an outsider and I think what caught people's attention about the club is the honesty and that you knew what you were going to get. It broke new ground and so did Factory, Peter [Hook] was always trying to sign new acts and some of the bands that played at the club were insane. Real recognise real at the end of the day. It wasn't about egos or pay cheques, and that's why it has such a massive legacy.

Above // 808 State.

Opposite // Tony Wilson at the Haçienda in May 1985.

Above // Rob Gretton, pictured in 1984 with girlfriend Lesley Gilbert. **Andrew 'Fletch' Fletcher**: "I think you've got to give credit to the original people who started it, like Tony Wilson, Rob Gretton and Alan Erasmus. Those guys created the blueprint."

Above and opposite // The early years of the club were characterised by performances from bands and musical artists, covering the full spectrum of sounds from punk to indie to spoken word and beyond. The gigs were a crucial part of the local cultural scene, attended by fans and bands alike – note The Durutti Column's Vini Reilly (far right).

Graeme Park is a DJ. He had a nine-year residency at the club.

Melanie Williams is a singer. Her vocals featured on the Sub Sub single "Ain't No Love (Ain't No Use)".

Graeme: The first time that I went I was working in a record shop in Nottingham. As a massive Factory Records fan, I heard that they were opening a nightclub and rather than wait for bands to come to Nottingham, if a band I wanted to see were on I'd get a train to the club.

Fast forward a few years to 1987 and I had become a DJ there. I met Mike Pickering at an *i-D* magazine photoshoot in London. I was aware of him because of his connection with Factory Records and we became friends. We put a night on in February 1988 and a few months later he called me and asked if I wanted to cover Friday night while he was on holiday – obviously I said that I'd love to, but he said that I had to come to the club immediately.

When I went in again it was May '88 and it was a completely different club. First of all, it was packed and it was hot and sweaty. Everyone was wearing this bizarre combination of dungarees, baggy jeans, acid-wash t-shirts and bandanas.

I went up the stairs to the DJ booth and suddenly I became aware that everyone had a mad look in their eyes. Someone offered me half a pill and told me to go and dance. Twenty minutes later I was downstairs and 'The Party' by Craze came on and I started getting the tingling – that's when I realised why Mike had told me to come early. I covered the Fridays for three weeks after that and those are the nights that I remember the most.

When Mike got back I got a call to say that they wanted me back to do it every week with him and then that was it, every single week until it closed.

Melanie: I always struggled with my mental health and the club became a form of therapy for me. I was having a terrible time with depression when my writing partner, Eric Goodman, dragged me along. I was stood on the balcony and suddenly Graeme Park's remix of 'Ain't No Love' came on. I'd never heard it in a club before – it was incredible.

I didn't really understand the enormity of what was happening and the impact until my friends came over from Australia and asked if we could go. It was an amazing privilege to play there.

Graeme: It didn't matter who you were, it was the first kind of club that was totally inclusive. Whether you were a barrister, a builder or a football hooligan, there was no aggro. Everyone was completely loved up and the music matched the vibe that everyone had.

Melanie: The impact on me was enormous. The '90s has become an iconic era and that has so much to do with what came out of the Haçienda. There was an authentic celebration of music in there. The gift was that you could feel good about who you were and about your uniqueness.

I used to wear my hair in long plaits, and I remember wearing a white velvet suit around that time too. I had my own sense of style and felt completely comfortable to express it.

I was blown away by some of the styles I saw in the club. It was like watching a movie full of unique characters and you had your own unique part to play in the story too. It was such a whirlpool full of amazing energy. It was totally inspirational.

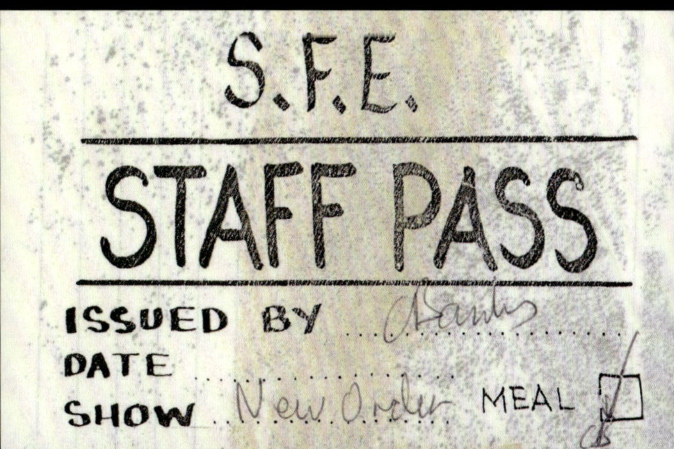

Above // Haçienda mementoes, including a fashion show as well as meal tickets for the club's on-site kitchen, La Cocina. **Anthony Crank**: "The Haçienda was a portal into another world. I remember seeing the photographs of Madonna. I couldn't believe they sold chips and gravy in there as well, in that little café."

1986-

1988

By 1986, Britain felt like a divided country. While "Loadsamoney" southerners, rich on free enterprise, taunted the poor, the north of England was suffering its highest unemployment rate since WWII. For the metropolitan elite of London, Manchester's image remained clouded in soot.

Into this ultimately blinkered mindset, it was club culture – that wonderful, sometimes idealised melting pot of race, gender and sexuality – which soothed the soul and sent worries packing. London had The Wag, Taboo and Café de Paris, all slavish devotees of style, served up in magazines like *The Face* and *i-D* magazine as the last word in nocturnal glamour. The Smoke's bright young things swished and twirled, albeit rather self-consciously, searching for flashbulbs like manic fashion sparrows. In contrast, up on Whitworth Street, money might have been too tight to mention, but the Haçienda was developing into an egalitarian playpen where everyone was welcome.

After years of hapless chancing, the club attempted to shed its image of "It'll be alright on the night". New manager Paul Mason, a man described by Peter Hook as "quiet and studious", was employed to instill order where there had been chaos. What the Haçienda needed were regular nights – identifiable themed weekly events where local students, still moping around in raincoats, could throw their homework on the fire and zone out to the Bunnymen. Temperance, run by future author Dave Haslam, proved to be a hit. Literature undergraduates, high on Keats and Yeats, were bussed in from campus to club, much to the delight of Tony Wilson, who at his heart craved an everyman approach to entry. Haslam dropped The Smiths next to Mantronix – steering a path for the indie/dance crossover that would dominate the club in the next few years.

A decade on from the infamous "I was there" Sex Pistols gig at the Lesser Free Trade Hall, things were moving on in Manchester. That infamous touch-light experience, witnessed by the city's finest, including New Order, Tony Wilson, Rob Gretton and Morrissey, was a pivotal moment that the city felt like commemorating. The Festival of the Tenth Summer – a week of events, including a concert at the G-Mex Centre, neatly crystallised the emerging scene. The Haçienda, basking in the afterglow, started to turn a profit.

Chad Jackson continued his Saturday night "Big Noise" residency, privy to the climatic changes happening below him on the dancefloor. "The whole atmosphere of the place, the clientele, everything, suddenly felt remarkably free and easy. There was no bad attitude, no thuggery. This is on the cusp of house, but before the drug thing started, which absolutely changed everything. It was a period of flux – exciting and groundbreaking – with so much potential."

"I wanted to totally reverse the door policy," says Mike Pickering. "When we did a party for *i-D* magazine in 1986, I asked Tony and Rob if we should make it free for the unemployed and nurses. If anyone was wearing Adidas Gazelles or baggy jeans, they'd get in free too. Within two or three weeks we had 1,600 people in a 1,200-capacity club. It was black and white, split down the middle, and it looked and felt absolutely fucking brilliant. Obviously the beginning of '88 was mind-blowing, and by '89 we could obviously play a wider range of music. But the beginning was wonderful. These were the golden years."

The *i-D* party, as reported by photographer Dave Swindells, was a neat turning point in the culture at large. Few travelled up from London that night, but appreciative style mavens from surrounding cities lapped up the magazine's advice and hit the club, donning BodyMap and Jean Paul Gaultier. This was the era of Swing Out Sister and Johnny Hates Jazz, but rhythmic rumbles – 'Trapped' by Colonel Abrams, Nitro Deluxe's 'This Brutal House' – began to infiltrate both taste and tempo.

03

i-D editor Alix Sharkey remembers the night well. "I was seriously impressed with the venue," he says, "but intimidated too. I arrived with Dylan Jones and Kate Fleet, all dressed up in our Ray Petri-inspired 'Buffalo' looks, and we were met with some disdain from the locals. It was hotter than July in there, absolutely sweltering, but the atmosphere was beyond cool. It definitely taught us that not everything revolved around our stylish London bubble."

In Swindells' accompanying photos, a young clubber called Jonathan thinks London is "Awful". "If you talk to someone on the Tube they think you're a rapist," he opines. Over in the corner, Ashley and Beverly, two hairdressers from Altrincham, are, in a rather forward-thinking way, wearing clothes by Christopher Nemeth and Judy Blame. Talk is of a DJ called Graeme, from the Garage in Nottingham. "He's an excellent mixer," they enthuse. An opinion that would be shared by many in the years to follow.

In sweet harmony, the issue also contained a lengthy feature by writer Simon Witter on the emergence of something called "House music", a new disco variant coming out of Chicago that promised to be the next big thing. "When the house music monster appeared, it was like a juggernaut that just hit the place," says Chad Jackson. "For a lot of us, the music fans who had gone from northern soul to jazz funk and then hip-hop, it was merely a continuation of good music. What I really liked about the Haçienda was the way they just left everyone to their own devices. DJs could be quite experimental. They could go out on the limb if they really felt passionate about a track. It felt like something was really happening."

By 1987, the Haçienda, increasingly namechecked by the style press, had developed into Manchester's most talked-about nightclub. The idea of three core nights – Thursday, Friday and Saturday – brought stability, and the city, emboldened by a new confidence, transformed itself into a destination location. Mike Pickering's Nude night thrived, with both Spin Inn and Eastern Bloc records providing the tunes that would soundtrack this quiet revolution. "Can you feel it", asked Mr Fingers, one of many "jacking tracks" of this early period. "Yes we can!" came the overwhelmingly positive response. Nothing would ever be quite the same again.

High on hope and its 4/4 purity, the club was convinced Chicago House was the way forward. Booking producers and DJs for their first UK gigs, Mike Pickering invited future luminaries, including Frankie Knuckles, Adonis and Larry Heard, across the pond. "The Haçienda was their introduction to England. That was the first time they'd ever been. There were 1,600 people packed in that Friday night," he remembers. "Frankie was nearly crying. He said, 'I can't believe that people outside my ghetto even know about this.' I said, well, look at the love for you out there. It's real, and it's happening. America hadn't got a clue, but Manchester was on it from the get-go."

House music, and its squelching Acid offshoot, irrefutably changed the club, but not everyone wanted in. Paul Cons' Zumbar night was an inspired antidote – described by the ideas-heavy promoter as an "adventurous mix of live entertainment, fashion and disco". Deftly blending art, comedy and music, Zumbar was cabaret with a capital C, a night that threw up leftfield appearances as disparate as politically incorrect comic Jerry Sadowitz, and *Coronation Street*'s Vera Duckworth. If that sounds incredulous, it's easy to forget that behind the scenes, things rarely went to plan. On New Year's Eve 1987, the club's takings – over £5,000 in bank notes – inexplicably caught alight and perished in the basement. Fighting fire with fire would continue to be a dominant theme.

Left // In 1986, Paul Cons joined the club as Entertainment and Promotions Manager, running the nights as the club slowly began to see a shift away from one-off gigs and shows and towards more defined club nights.

Opposite // Nude had already begun on Friday nights in 1985 and was to become a focal point in the club's weekly schedule.

EVERY FRIDAY
NUDE NIGHT
HOUSE, HIP HOP
FUNK · DJ—MP²
FREE
before 12·00
with this invite
Fac 51 The Haçienda
11/13 Whitworth St West
Manchester
Tel 061 236 5051

EVERY
FRIDAY
NUDE
NIGHT
ELECTRO · SOUL · FUNK
REGGAE — DJ:MP²
NOW £1·50 BEFORE 11PM!
(£1·00 UB40 NUS)
THE HACIENDA 11/13 WHITWORTH ST WEST MANCHESTER TEL 061 236 5051

EVERY
FRIDAY
NUDE
NIGHT
ELECTRO · SOUL · FUNK
REGGAE — DJ:MP²
ADMISSION: £1·50 BEFORE 11PM (£1·00 UB40 NUS)
£2·00 AFTER 11PM (£1·50 UB40 NUS)
THE HACIENDA 11/13 WHITWORTH ST WEST MANCHESTER TEL 061 236 5051

> You've got to remember that everyone thought we were weirdos at the time. We didn't want proper jobs. I didn't give a shit because I had no future anyway, and no qualifications, so I thought, 'I'll do exactly what I want and something that's worthwhile'. We felt like we were helping to resurrect Manchester.

Mike Pickering

Opposite // Mike Pickering and Martin Prendergast – also known as Little Martin – DJed as MP^2 at Friday's Nude night.

Mark XTC is a former Haçienda DJ.

I was 17 when I first went. I entered a scratching/mixing DJ competition, which I ended up winning. That's how I started going to the club more often, it was a wild experience.

I worked in a record shop in town, and I used to sell records to people like Graeme [Park], so I made a lot of friends from the club that way too.

London didn't have the iconic rave culture that Manchester had. It was miles bigger here, and much more anthemic. Everyone would have their hands in the air, completely lost in the music.

At the time, I was a lot more hip-hop orientated, so I'd wear Jordans (that I still wear now) and caps. A lot of other people had the baggy t-shirt and fluorescent t-shirt vibe, and they'd do their rave dancing, whilst I was doing the hip-hop dancing. It mingled and then it quickly became both, the cultures matched and linked.

The Haçienda was a melting pot of people from all different backgrounds and cultures. People are still friends from back then now and still go out raving!

When I was working in the record shops, people would come and listen to records that they'd heard in the club over and over again just to reminisce and feel the buzz that they'd felt there. Everyone just wanted to recall what they'd heard.

The music opened up so much to so many different people. It was completely multicultural.

I made music and still make music now for people to dance to. When I'd hear what was going off on the dancefloor, I knew that that was what I wanted to put into my own tracks.

Opposite and following pages // Nights at the Haç. **Chad Jackson**: "The crowd was very mixed. I've always been the sort of person that believes in equality, whether that's race or sexuality, so I really respected the fact the club had a healthy mix. As long as you weren't causing a disturbance you were allowed in. A lot of clubs in those days wouldn't let Black people in, which was nonsense. It was a different world back then."

NUDE
FUNK

EMERGENCY
EXIT

S.S.

Above left // Club-goer Dave Spence's original membership card, signed by a host of names connected to the Haç, including Tony Wilson, Ben Kelly, Peter Saville, DJs and members of New Order, Stone Roses, Happy Mondays, The Smiths and Inspiral Carpets.

Above right // Kicking off in May 1986, indie night Temperance was the first truly successful student-aimed night at the club, under DJ Dave Haslam.

Opposite // Dance troupe Foot Patrol at the Haçienda in 1988.

Right // Resident DJ Mike Pickering was an influential figure in shaping the club's sound.

> We'd stand on the barren dancefloor of the Haçienda, jerking and ticking like teenage robots. No one is looking at you, but secretly you'd hope someone might steal a glance at your moves. At the Haçienda, I always thought I was in some kind of futurist amphitheatre, where the world is looking on, applauding my modernity.

Darren Harcourt

NUMERO
UNO

OE
7" Docs
AL 2
STER 13

This page and opposite // Two *i-D* parties were held at the Haçienda, the first on 14 June 1986, attended by the magazine's editor, Dylan Jones. It's been claimed that this night was the first time that 'rain' fell down on the punters in the form of sweat condensing on the club's glass ceiling, because it had never been so busy.

Opposite and above // Justin Robertson: "I remember going to the *i-D* party in 1986. By the end of the evening everything had changed for me, literally overnight."

Overleaf // In 1986, Factory Records commissioned an artwork by David Mach for an installation at the Haçienda, made up of thousands of 12" singles of New Order's 'Confusion' stacked around the club's central pillars. **Paul Cons**: "It didn't get that much of a response at the time, but it was an incredible work of art, the kind of thing that would get loads of attention now."

In Conversation

John Cooper Clarke is a poet and performer.

Peter Hook is a musician and co-owner of the Haçienda.

Bruce Mitchell is a member of post-punk band The Durutti Column.

JCC: Why did the Haçienda work so well? If I had the kind of nose that could make that happen, I'd be pissing pure gold right now. That kind of entrepreneurial expertise belongs to the likes of Tony Wilson.

Peter: I didn't even know what the fuck was happening. I didn't know I was financing it. What I liked about it, though, was that it gave oddballs like us somewhere to go.

JCC: Where it was built, that part of town, there wasn't really much going on there before the club arrived. It was all neglected industrial premises that hadn't been used for years. Probably what they'd call "steam punk" now.

Peter: What always amused me was that it was a fucking yacht showroom before. When Tony took me and Rob to see it, I was more amazed that there was somewhere in Manchester that sold yachts. I couldn't believe that he was going to turn it into a club.

The thing that was interesting was that we would go to there and feel safe, totally cut off from the outside world and reality. I remember the first trouble there ever was in the Haçienda was when Martin Hannett's girlfriend tried to stab him. That was the only trouble. At that point, we even kept the trouble in-house.

JCC: I heard Joy Division's famous albums in the process of manufacture, because in them days it was on cassettes and Martin was driving me around at the same time as he was producing Joy Division.

Peter: Martin made us three look normal. He was absolutely fucking barmy. His big beef about what we did, by Tony and Rob opening a club, was that he felt it wasn't fuelling our industry. He felt that we should have been looking after our industry by making a recording studio.

The thing I loved about Tony and Rob was that they weren't particularly bothered about us and what we thought. They were bothered about every oddball in Manchester, they wanted to look after everybody, and that was the strange thing about it. It was like a youth club for loonies.

JCC: I was more of a habitué of the Russell Club when it was the Factory, over in Hulme on the edge of Moss Side. It began as a bus workers' social club and they would have people like Winston Groovy on, mainly West Indian acts, but Iggy Pop played there too. It was another club that was safe as houses.

Bruce: That's where music lived at that time.

Peter: Tony tried to take that to the Haçienda.

JCC: What I'm trying to say is that it turned into a different thing then. Because there was no warning of house music and things like that. The first I ever heard about all that area was at the Haçienda and via Peter [Hook] and Tony [Wilson]. I didn't see it develop, I didn't see it coming from going to the Russell Club. They were entirely separate places, the Russell Club was a rock venue like any other. A bit of dope, the odd theft. That's what I remember.

Bruce: I was hanging out and doing whatever I could be helpful with. It was absolutely right for its time, even a little bit ahead of its time, and driven by unusual characters and music.

Peter: People used to say to me "you can't buy a legacy like this", and I'd say "you'd have a fucking good go, mate". We were all skint for years and had no idea that we were funding it over £10,000 a month. But would we swap it? No way.

Bruce: Tony Wilson used to say, "We're not here to make money, we're here to make history" and I think that says it all.

JCC: History is littered with broke people.

Peter: So many people were inspired by the bedrock that we had, through us working through punk and all the rest of it, our career. What we built with the club, it went on to influence so many people. People walked out and saw what they wanted to do in life. And that's exactly what happened to us when we left the Sex Pistols' gig.

JCC: No one man could invent those events in the order that they came in.

Bruce: It was an inspiration. The punters looked fantastic because they were reflecting their creativity. Everyone in there was touched by talent. The young people who were heading to the club were fired up. Who knows why, it happens to every generation that is in love with music and the things that spin from music.

Peter: In our crowd, when we began, there were several individuals; Bruce and John were two of the highly individual people.

Bruce: I remember the way Carol Morley used to do her outfits. The hat and the alligator on a stick. There really was a look about those characters.

Peter: They'd dress up and make the most of it and that was what was wonderful. Then it went through that period when the house music took over and it was packed. That made a big change in all the wonderful people that we'd used to see, like John Cale and Jonathan Richman who, when he played, he insisted on having no PA and just an acoustic guitar. They just weren't there anymore. As the club nights took off we lost those wacky intimate gigs that were very special to us 'live' music people. Ironically, though, I ended up loving both.

JCC: I remember that – he wanted to recreate a village hall. No showbiz at all. He was a genius that guy. But the acid house movement was, in a way, what gave it its international reach. When you say Haçienda to people now, that's what they'll think of before anything else.

Peter: Up to that point the fashion was in-house. Everyone was expressing themselves and then when you got to acid house the fashion came in with it. The way those kids were dressing, it didn't evolve from the club, it evolved from Ibiza and London. Before that, it was strictly for the people of Manchester that came from the same background.

Bruce: It was a bit like an arts centre on acid.

Z

Opposite // Fire-eater and all-round entertainer The Great Orshanti wows the crowds at new night Zumbar, which featured a host of performers working the northern club circuit and introduced them to a younger crowd, who embraced the camp air of old-fashioned entertainment for several years, before it made way for the rave scene that was to follow.

Above right // *Coronation Street*'s Vera Duckworth, otherwise known as Liz Dawn, was near royalty on the northern club scene, and played the part to perfection, arriving in a limo and wearing a fur coat. She went down a storm.

Above // Miss Zumbar 1988 saw the club host a beauty pageant in its own unique style.

Opposite // **Dave Wilson** remembers his appearance at Karry-on Karaoke in 1988: "Karaoke was yet to become the cultural phenomenon we know it to be today, so when the Zumbar night started a weekly competition in The Gay Traitor bar it was a proper curiosity. One night, probably slightly worse for wear, my mate Geraldine and I decided to give it a go. We sang – and I use the term in the loosest sense – Barry Manilow's 'Copacabana', had a laugh, won and gave the whole thing barely a second thought.

A few weeks later, however, we were contacted and told that we were through to the Grand Final, to be held upstairs, on the main stage! I took some persuading but we agreed and all our mates came along. We were second to last on. The club was heaving. I sellotaped the lyrics to my wrist and took to the stage, resplendent in a sailor t-shirt from Geese (Geraldine looked amazing in a leopard skin dress). Our four minutes on stage were a blur. We were awful. And we won! We were presented with our prize, a case of Factory wine, with beautifully designed Peter Saville labels and their own Fac number, if I remember rightly. Probably worth an absolute fortune today but we drank the lot within a week."

Polyfilla

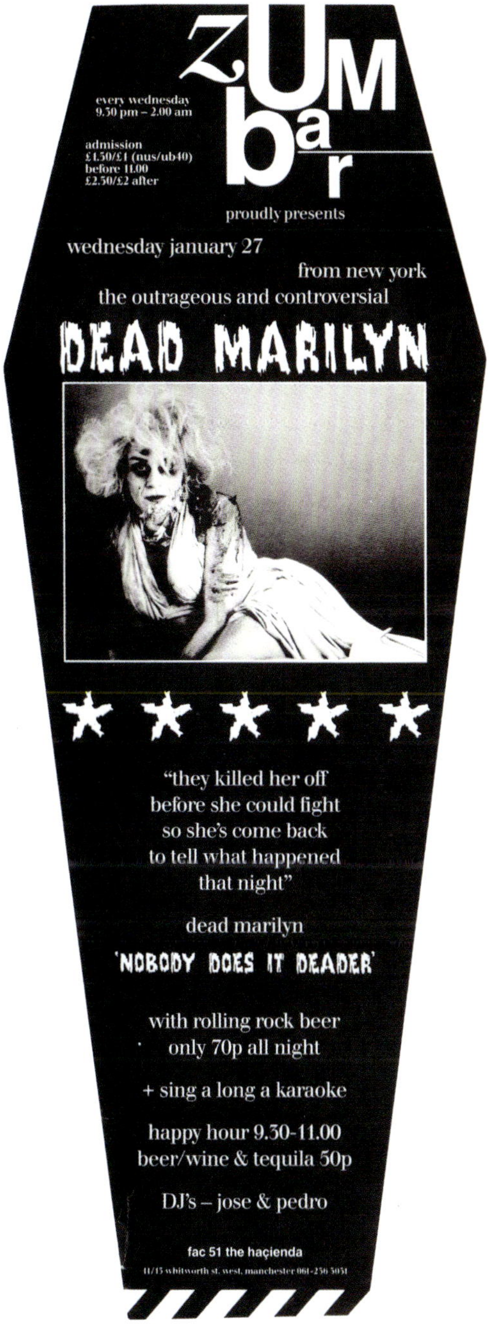

Previous page // The beauty pageant, held on Zumbar's final ever night. Clearly an emotional affair.

Opposite // The club's second *i-D* party, held on 6 July 1988 and known as The *i-D* World Tour, saw Mark Moore DJ and a performance from Zara Stockbridge, model and muse to designer Vivenne Westwood.

This page // 'Nobody does it deader.' A Zumbar appearance from Dead Marilyn, an American club performer whose character was based on Marilyn Monroe beyond the grave.

Above and opposite // The opening night of Hot, a night originally intended to act as the summer season of Zumbar, but which was later caught up in the explosion of the rave scene. The first night saw a swimming pool – which later burst – installed in the club, and a wheel which was spun at midnight and dictated the price of booze for the next hour. **Paul Cons**: "I remember standing in the DJ booth with Tony Wilson when the wheel landed on the FREE BAR! section. After a moment's silence we saw a stampede to the bar. Needless to say it didn't go down that well, and they quietly removed the free bar section after that."

HALF PRICE LAGER AND WINE
DOUBLES FOR THE PRICE OF SINGLES
FUCK OFF !
FREE BAR !
20p OFF THE LOT

Roger Sanchez is a DJ. He first played at the Haçienda in 1993.

I first started coming over to the UK when the early house and rave scene began to explode around the world. Coming from the New York City clubs and underground scene, I first started playing in clubs up north in Scotland, Blackpool of all places, and London, and then shortly after at the Haçienda when it started to become a mecca for house music in the UK.

It was the early euphoric piano house that translated really well with what I was playing at the time; I connected with it instantly. The club was a real introduction to the movement that was happening in the UK, and my kind of American, soulful house sound merged with it very well.

At that point in time it had the closest atmosphere to the underground clubs of New York City, but there were very distinct British crowds that were really into the music and the rave-oriented sense of euphoria. Tracks would drop and people would lose their minds on the floor, which reminded me of certain places I was playing in New York. That was the commonality. It was also very inclusive, and that mirrored back to what was going on in New York, too.

The first time I ever played there was with Frankie Knuckles, David Morales and Graeme Park. I remember walking up to the booth that was on the right side overlooking the dancefloor and it reminded me of the Tunnel in New York City – the brick walls and the long, rectangular room. The sound was fantastic. The energy was electric. People had their hands in the air.

The whole acid house smiley face is the style that I remember most. And people dressed like workers, with reflective panelling and a lot of orange and green, like they were about to pull you over to do some work in the middle of the road. It was similar to the States in the sense that a lot of people were wearing baggy pants and there were quite a few shirtless men flying about, but the smiley face, UK rave aesthetic was really taking over. There were a lot of glowsticks and whistles, too.

I was dressed in a lot of black at that time, a very New York vibe. I wore a lot of Kangol and the classic black Adidas tracksuit, too. I was very much a combination of the hip-hop style because that's where my roots are, I enjoyed wearing a bit of denim and the shell-toe Adidas trainers. Even though I wasn't from here, I felt like my style resonated a lot with the movement in the UK.

I think the UK was influenced by what we were doing in New York, specifically the house scene, but there were a lot of sounds from the UK that I began to integrate into my sets. A big one was the euphoric piano that immediately got hands in the air. And then the diva vocals became a bigger thing in the UK than in the States and that started to enter not only the music that I played, but the music that I produced too.

I equated the scene at the time to the same types of venues like Paradise Garage in New York City and Zanzibar in New Jersey. All these clubs I equated with what was happening here in Manchester. The Haçienda was first up, and I knew it was an incredibly important venue in the UK, so it felt really important to be here.

What's interesting is that I see music as very cyclical. That rave generation was incredibly unique and now many of us have grown up and had kids; kids that are now raving themselves. So, as opposed to what our parents did, they didn't have that kind of activity. For us, going to a club or going to a rave is a very recognisable part of our culture. The fact that it has now come back around and been embraced so widely by the younger generation is great. You see younger and older people raving together so often at events now, and that's what's special about this music.

The music of that time was really fresh and unique and what we're seeing now is that those sounds are being recycled and reinterpreted with this generation.

Depending on how much time I had before doing a show I would usually go to the record shop, because at the time we were playing on vinyl. I would've also organised my records for the evening, put them into alphabetical order and the different sounds. I kept everything very organised because when it was time for me to play,

I knew exactly where everything was. Then I'd get to the club, and before I went on I'd always check out who else was playing and map in my head where I'd want to take the crowd with my set.

The sound system was very organic. It was definitely cavernous, too. Being on the floor is different to being in the booth. The booth had a really good sound, you could feel the bottom end from the floor and the clarity that was coming up to the booth from the floor. Unless you were on the floor you didn't really feel that, but the DJ booth was really well sonically organised. It was really cool.

For me, it was part of a larger picture in terms of the community of DJs, artists and club goers that I met. There was this community that stretched from the UK back to the States and then to Spain and it all felt very connected. But Manchester became a bit of a mecca because of the club. It set the tone for what was then going to take off, way before Ibiza became very popular.

It also set the tone for what tracks were going to explode in the UK club scene and then some of them even went on to become big radio records. I think that for me personally, it's that feeling of community and understanding the kind of club goers that were here in Manchester and their commonality to someone from London or Scotland, as well as the differences. The Haçienda set the bar for places like Cream in Liverpool; it allowed these super clubs to be born from what it embodied.

'Anthem' by N-Joi stands out as the defining moment for me. I remember playing that track and looking down at the strobes going off. The room was flashing black and white and everyone had their hands in the air, screaming when the piano hits. That was perfect to me.

Above // Paul Cons with bar manager Leroy Richardson. **Leroy Richardson:** "I started working at the club the year it opened, in 1982, collecting glasses."

Opposite // DJ David Morales, part of the wave of US DJs who came over to play the club.

The first time I ever played there was with Frankie Knuckles, David Morales and Graeme Park… The sound was fantastic. The energy was electric. People had their hands in the air.

Roger Sanchez

1988-

-1991

From the start of 1988, until time immemorial, the Haçienda inadvertently entered its imperial phase. Fuelled by the "wonder drug" ecstasy, acid house had proved a force to be reckoned with, although at the advent of the year this game-changing pill was still a fairly innocuous presence. By July, all that would change. The fast-approaching "Summer of Love" had chosen its hat and was coming out to play. For the majority of people passing through the club's doors in its sixth year, few would realise the transformative impact both MDMA and the venue would play in their lives.

Not only was the Haçienda a hit with the locals, but a steady stream of earnest young men arrived at the venue on a musical road to Damascus. The Chemical Brothers have often stated they felt explicitly inspired from the minute they entered the place; and they were not alone, the university choice for many students was dictated by the palpable vibe that shook the club's Victorian bricks on any given weekend. Manchester was the place to study, not only because of its renowned academic establishments, but because the Haçienda offered an alternative education, a curriculum offered nowhere else in the world.

Future DJ Justin Robertson was a self-confessed Factory nerd from the Home Counties. A naive boy studying Philosophy at Manchester University, he loved The Fall and A Certain Ratio, but he also loved reggae, Hawkwind and Tangerine Dream in equal measure. Working part time in the record store Eastern Bloc, Robertson was perfectly poised – right place, right time – to witness what was going on in the classroom of his dreams.

"When I first went to the Haçienda, Mike Pickering was playing things like Joyce Sims and Mantronix. It was like a baptism of fire. But later on, house music was the real backbone, and that really pricked up my ears. Funnily enough, it reminded me of Tangerine Dream – formless, unruly music that went on and on. That late '80s period was insane. Walking into the club was like being in the middle of a frenetic carnival. There were whistles blowing constantly, and all this really energetic dancing, like a block party kind of vibe.

"I didn't really take ecstasy to start with, but even without it there was a really weird feeling of togetherness. All the perceived snootiness that the Haçienda had, rightly or wrongly, simply faded away. At one point there were all these really smartly dressed people, those that worked in Geese, wearing designer jackets and drinking Japanese lager. All that disappeared overnight."

By June, New Order, acutely aware of dance music's potent force, were holed up in Ibiza, recording the album that would become *Technique*. The spiritual white island – long a haven for hippies, clubbers and thrill-seekers of all persuasions – was the perfect location to put down both roots and beats. The band were in thrall to its Balearic charm, as was most of the UK at this point. Dance music culture was gripping everything in its wake, seduced by ecstasy and that relentless 4/4 rhythm, which punctuated clubs from Burnley to Berlin, and everywhere in between.

Over in Manchester, the Haçienda was fast becoming one of the most revered clubs in the world. Bar manager Leroy Richardson, a long-term employee, remembers the transition from relative normality to something else entirely. "It was around this time when I first started seeing the drug influence, but on a very small scale. Ecstasy was only for a select few. To tell you the truth, nobody knew about it, apart from the ones that were doing it, most obviously the Happy Mondays and their pals. They just seemed to be having a really, really good time. If it was cocaine, you'd be thinking, my God, what's going on? But it was like, oh, it's a pill. So what?"

The Happy Mondays were an unlikely looking mob signed to Factory Records. Despite their shambolic image and scallywag demeanour, Tony Wilson, characteristically effusive, declared Shaun Ryder's lyrics as being "up there with Bob Dylan".

04

"When I saw them," says Leroy Richardson, "I couldn't work out where they came from. I don't mean physically, but how they had suddenly appeared at the Haçienda. One minute, they didn't exist, and the next they were there. I knew Tony had signed them but I thought, there's no way they can play their instruments. They looked dodgy. Put it this way, if they knocked on your door, you wouldn't have answered it."

In some ways, ecstasy's loved-up charm was the true catalyst for change. While its euphoric high promoted trance-like dancing, Richardson believes it was the levelling effect he witnessed that was more revolutionary. "You'd suddenly see all aspects of society within the club. There were nice middle-class girls mixing with your guys from housing estates and football fans. All life was there, just getting on with each other."

By 1989, things had reached a high that showed no signs of abating. Pickering and Park's Nude ruled the day, something not unnoticed by lofty American magazine *Newsweek*, which declared the Haçienda "the most famous club in the world".

"'89 to '91 was the golden period," says Graeme Park, whose fluid, life-affirming sets had become the stuff of legend. "Madchester was in full flow – this ridiculous mash-up of baggy bacchanalia, coupled with a fervour on the dancefloor, which was breathtaking in the extreme. Mike Pickering had asked me to visit the club, prior to it really kicking off. When I walked into the Haçienda, which was roasting, there were people in there wearing dungarees and bandanas, fellas with their shirts off. Everyone had this mad look in their eyes. I went to the DJ box, knocked on the door, and Mike was dressed this way as well. He gave me this massive hug, someone offered me a pill and the rest, as they say, is history."

"In retrospect, it sounds fantastic, and it was, but it all went sour really quickly for me," says Pickering. "I think it was the night we did Hitman and Her. That was the death knell for the club. Nothing to do with that show, but I saw some heavy violence that night, which I'd never witnessed in all the years the club had been open. Bouncers were getting hammered by gangs. There were millions of pounds of drugs being sold – and they're wonderful drugs – but the inevitability is, these guys are going to come in and tax us. I saw it coming. I was working-class Manchester. I knew what it was all about."

Despite the drawbacks, the city was in full swing. The Happy Mondays, together with The Stone Roses, characterised the period with a confident swagger, and the atmosphere the Haçienda engendered further cemented that simple but effective catchphrase: "Madchester".

"Mad for it" was less a question and more a statement of intent.

"Hedonism, coupled with intellectualism, that's what sums up the Haçienda for me at that point," says Paul Flynn. "I don't think you got the wholesale embrace of hedonism until ecstasy arrived. What the Haçienda housed, for that ecstasy moment, is a place at night where you're mixing the idea of entertainment with ideas. And what a magical combination it was."

But by 1990, increasingly beleaguered by its problems, the club was forced to temporarily close. The crowds, most of whom were oblivious to the problems, could have danced until the cows came home, but things were getting out of control, and the only way forward was to put a halt to proceedings.

"The Haçienda at this point was absolutely something else," says employee Anton Razak. "I've never seen anything like it. Watching Mike Pickering DJing, the adoration he got from the crowd, was incredible to see. You couldn't help but stand there and be in awe of what was going on. The music only stopped when the police were outside banging on the door, shouting to turn the music off. The crowd went mental. As did everything else. It could only go one way."

Oh, Madchester, so much to answer for.

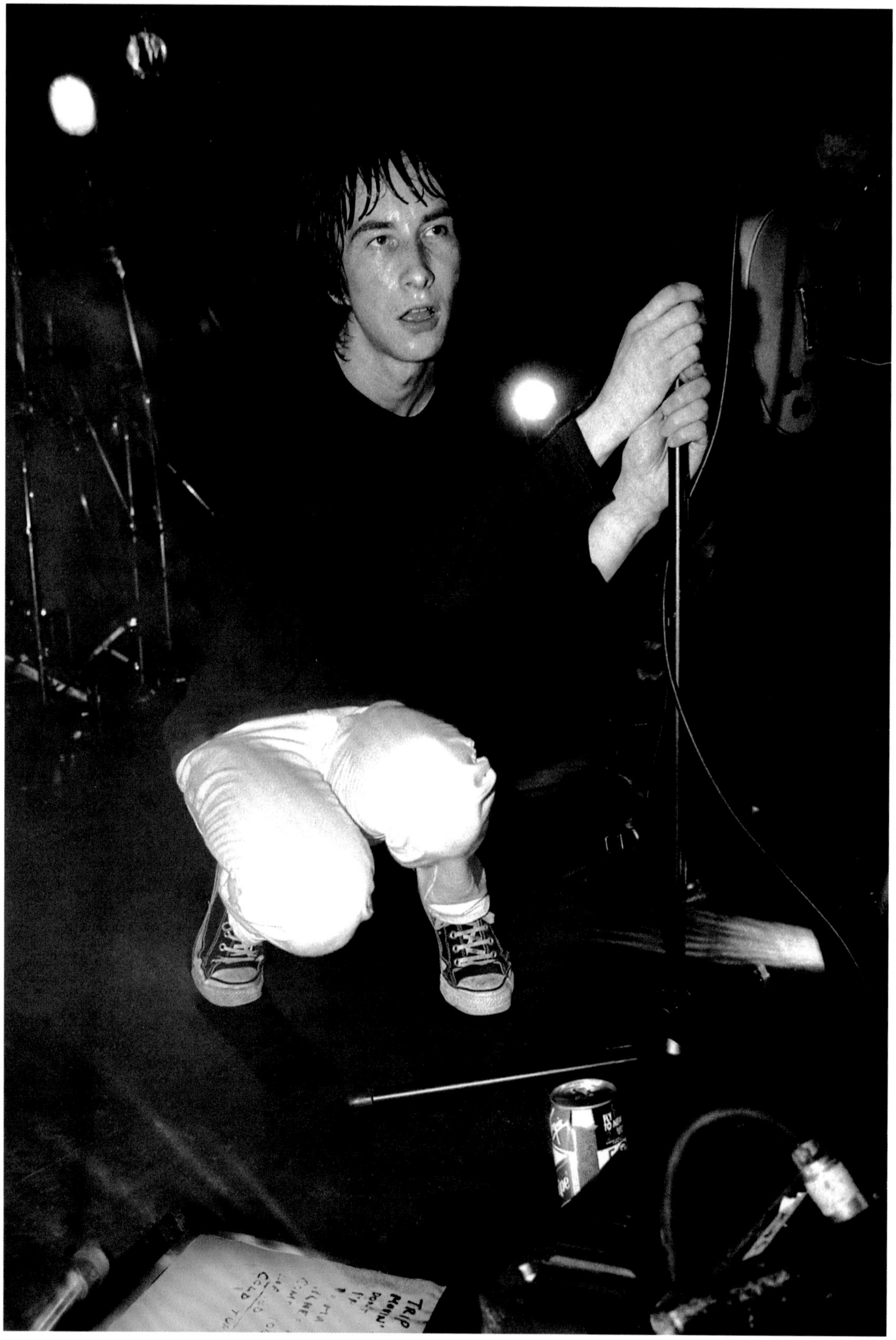

Above // Bobby Gillespie of Primal Scream, onstage during the band's performance at the Haçienda as part of the *Screamadelica* tour in 1991.

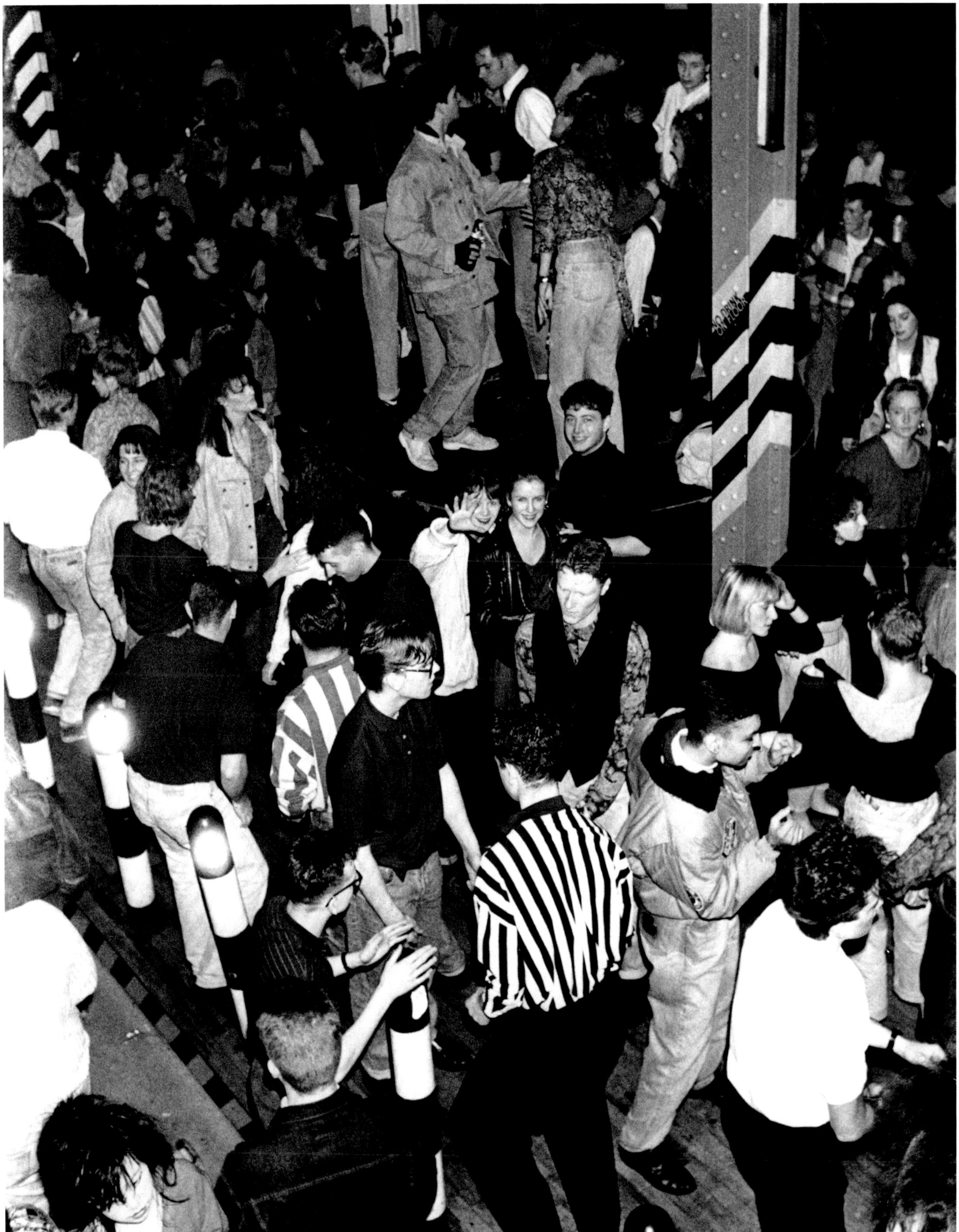
NO DRINK
ON FLOOR

Andrew O'Hagan is an award-winning novelist and non-fiction author. The Haçienda featured prominently in his acclaimed novel *Mayflies.*

Irvine Welsh is the author of novels including *Trainspotting* and *Filth*. He launched his book *Ecstasy* at the club in June 1996.

Andrew: I can still to this day remember how the group of boys I was friends with responded to the word "Haçienda". It was an absolute spirit of the age. When I first went it was everything I expected and hoped it would be and then more.

You felt like you were in a safe space for people who didn't give a fuck. There weren't many spaces for people who didn't give a fuck in the '80s. In fact, not giving a fuck was a capital offence. It was still a country dominated by wankery and hostility to the idea of the energy and freedoms that young people might care about, so the club felt like a gleaming place to go.

There was really something special and eccentric about it and I thought it was fucking magic from the beginning.

Irvine: You just walked into this amazing world. I was really impressed by it because I'd been to New York in the early '80s and I had become really interested in disco and electronic music and there was a lot of that at the club.

When the house period kicked off, I became absolutely obsessed with acid house. I was travelling to clubs up and down the country, but the place to go was the Haçienda, it was the perfect launch pad for acid house.

Andrew: It was a godsend for somebody like me because it opened up the post-punk sensibility on the dancefloor.

Irvine: It influenced all of my writing. I've had a long relationship with Manchester from the Northern Soul scene onwards and I never give it enough credit. The city was a massive influence on me and the people that I met there still have a big part to play in my life now.

Andrew: There was something really refreshing about the club fashion-wise as well. I felt that you could wear anything, whereas a lot of other places at the time felt quite dictatorial even if they advertised freedom. There was something in Manchester that if someone came up to you in a fur hat and a Hawaiian shirt it was suddenly cool.

Irvine: I think there was an interference, you had it with The Stone Roses and The [Happy] Mondays, with the casual football movement and acid house. It filtered down from the Man City and Man United cool cats who would do anything when it came to fashion. Then there'd be people in there dressed like David Byrne or like their grandfather, there was a kind of permissiveness about it.

Andrew: When you went through those doors it just felt like ground zero international coolness.

Irvine: It must be up there with the very best clubs in the world, and there are very few clubs in Britain that have done that. It's the tie-in with Factory [Records] and the visionary that Tony [Wilson] was. It has a mad, cultural resonance because it started before acid house, so it somehow feels like an even bigger movement.

Andrew: It wasn't the kind of place that was defined by club nights. It was FAC51, the building was a piece of art, the concept of the place was a piece of art, its identity went over and above the music.

Irvine: Thatcher's Britain was drab and depressing and the Haçienda almost felt like a defiant launchpad from post-industrial Manchester that took everyone into a whole new era.

Andrew: The thing about the post-industrial look about the place – the yellow, the black, the use of metal, iron, chevrons and road signs – was that it was always stuff that was supposed to be cold to the touch, industrial and a bit clinical, but actually the genius of it, the way that it was conceived by Wilson and Pete Saville, meant that it created a new warmth, even though you were encased in this almost skeletal post-industrial wasteland.

Irvine: The social class thing to me was very important, because from Northern Soul to disco it was all working-class kids who were steeped in that environment.

Andrew: We looked after each other in a club context in a way that is really unusual across the rest of your life. It was a perfect microcosm, but people did really look after each other in there, you felt like you'd met people who actually gave a fuck about you.

Irvine: As acid house and ecstasy kicked in, you became so connected with the beat and club movement. If felt like you were doing something really clandestine. You had a lot of these nice straight kids who would normally just go out and have a few drinks suddenly going out and taking illegal class A drugs, so they were criminalised by society.

Andrew: The people who went to clubs like the Haçienda were going at life differently. They changed the world, and they never get the credit for it. The moral majority was trying to get those clubs shut because the future was being forged in the walls.

New values were being forced in clubs, not at political party conferences. Those clubs were throwing out new ideas and new values, which you could see lighting up the country during the mid- to late '80s and into the '90s.

In the mid-'80s we all wore white t-shirts, black leather jackets and jeans turned up at the bottom, which was post-punk/indie boy gear. Then at the Haçienda all the contrast and colour went up.

Irvine: When I was going out during the acid house scene I had this big Himalayan wool jacket that I used to love wearing in the winter. As I was coming up, I'd wrap myself up in the jacket to conserve every bit of heat and get the full impact, and then rip it off like a sort of butterfly.

The whole process of going to the club – the interactions that you would have, the people you'd meet – so much of it has to do with the music. I got absolutely immersed in dance music, I bought decks and started DJing, but I found that when I was writing I wanted to replicate the beats and effects of house music on the page.

By doing this I was trying to replicate the excitement and youth of what I was experiencing when I was going out. The club was a massive practical influence to me, rather than just in terms of content. It was a conscious attempt to look at the process of writing and how an acid-house sensibility could be filtered through.

I think when something as seismic as that happens in your own cultural lifetime it's something that you have to engage with if you're any kind of artist at all. You have to engage with that reality and the significance and power of it.

Opposite // On the podium of the main dancefloor, 1988.

Above // Temperance, 1990.

Opposite and above // Clubbers and performers from the dance group Foot Patrol dance in 1990, as the Haçienda begins to move away from gigs and entertainment and towards the dance music scene.

Above // Before long, Hot became completely consumed by the acid house and rave scene.

Above // Hot was very busy and, true to its name, very hot. The club would buy up the entire stock of ice pops from the wholesalers of Manchester and give them out for free.

Opposite // The club's sixth birthday party had a haunted house theme. A bridge was built over the canal at the rear of the club to give access to a ghost train. Previous Zumbar performer Dead Marilyn made another appearance.

FAC 51 THE
HAÇIENDA
SATURDAY
MAY 21 1988
THE SIXTH
BIRTHDAY

FRIDAY 29/4/88

11.00	CHECK THIS OUT (CUBAN)	L.A. MIX
	MAGIC FEET	MIKE DUNNE
	WIGGIN'	MAYDAY
	JACK IT ALL NIGHT LONG	BAD BOY BILL
	COMMUNICATE	FULL HOUSE
	I CANT WAIT	JOE CHURCH
	IF YOU SHOULD NEED A FRIEND	BLAZE
	WHERE DID YOUR LOVE GO?	E'LEESA
	B Y MY SIDE (JONESY'S)	CHARLENE
11-30	THE LOVE I LOST (HITMAN'S)	M. IMPERIAL
	JUST WANT ANOTHER CHANCE	REESE
	TASTE MY LOVE	KYM MAZELLE
	DIRTY TALK (USA)	KLEIN + M.B.O.
	AL-NAAFISH	HASHIM
	ALRIGHT x 2	MASTERS AT WORK
	SING A SONG	MANTRONIX
	UGLY PEOPLE BE QUIET	CASH MONEY
	RUN'S HOUSE	RUN D.M.C.
12.00	MOVE YOUR BODY	M. JEFFERSON
	TO THE BEAT OF THE DRUM	WIRED
	FORCE FIELD	REESE + SANTONIO
	GROOVE THAT WONT STOP	K. SAUNDERSON
	HOW TO PLAY OUR MUSIC	REESE + SANTONIO
	HOUSE REACTION (MAYHEM)	T CUT F
	DO YOU WANNA DANCE?	T. BALDWIN
	am a DOG	Dancer
	GET THE BUG (INST)	PIERRE'S F.C.
12.20	P.A. BY "BLOW"	
12.35	SIT ON THE FACE	H.M. BALDWIN
	MAGIC FEET	MIKE DUNNE

Time	Track	Artist
12.45	ACID OVER	TYREE
	GIVE IT TO ME	BAM BAM
	DONT LEAD ME	M.M. BALDWIN
	PARTY PEOPLE	ROYAL HOUSE
	A DAY IN THE LIFE	BLACK RIOT
	THE SOUND (MAYDAY)	REESE + SANTONIO
	WIGGIN'	MAYDAY
1.00	MUSIC TAKES U AWAY	L'IL LOUIS
	AND THE BREAK GOES ON	BREAK BOYZ
	IT TAKES TWO	ROB BASE
	GOODFOOT	D.MOET + EX.CALIBER
	JACK THE RIPPER	L.L. COOL J.
	DMC. LET THE MUSIC PLAY	STETSASONIC
	RAW	BIG DADDY KANE
	SUPER CASANOVA	SUPER LOVER + CASANOVA
	I FEEL IT	SUZIE + CUBANS
1.30	FALLOUT	MORNING AFTER
	PRIVATE PARTY	WALLY JUMP JNR.
	RIGHT BACK TO YOU	TEN CITY
	A LOVE SUPREME (CHASIN')	WILL DOWNING
	LOST IN THE SOUND	ADONIS
	CAN YOU FEEL IT	M.R. FINGERS
	R U HOT ENUFF	VIRGO
	THANK YA	SWEET D
	CAN U DANCE	KENNY JASON.
2.00	SOMEDAY	CE CE ROGERS

Previous pages // Mike Pickering's playlist from a Friday night Nude in April 1988.

Left // Temperance Club hits the road, as the Haçienda took the night to the Locomotive Club in Paris. Bands and DJs would make the trip, including Peter Hook's band Revenge and Inspiral Carpets.

Opposite // Inspiral Carpets in Paris, alongside band member Clint Boon's membership card to the club.

FAC51
THE HACIENDA

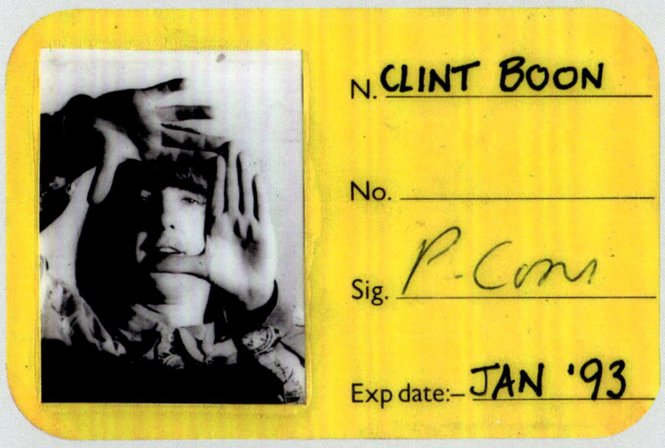
N. CLINT BOON
No.
Sig.
Exp date:– JAN '93

Left (top) // Dry Bar, a standalone venue opened by the Haçienda in Manchester's Northern Quarter.

Left (middle) // Ben Kelly (left) in Dry Bar, which he designed. With Peter Hook (right).

Left (bottom) and opposite // Clubbers on the Haçienda dancefloor.

Above and opposite // DJ Graeme Park.

RoXY
DOUBLE
TROUBLE
THE
REBEL MC

Jon Dasilva is a DJ, producer and former resident DJ at the club.

I first went to the club in 1983/84. It was a brilliant venue that always had brilliant line-ups, and I would come over from Preston to watch bands play there.

I moved back up north in January 1988 for university with the idea of setting up an arts centre and doing my own clubs. I was hanging out at the Haçienda during that time because my best mate got a job behind the bar, and I'd got to know Laurent Garnier in that process.

I got picked up within a couple of months and then I was totally subsumed in the club. It was exhilarating, I'm a huge Factory Records fan and that fed into Manchester as a city and the aura.

It was very difficult in those days to find a club that played pure house, it was usually in gay clubs that you'd see some of the big Chicago stars of that time coming over, but the Haçienda was leading that in the north.

The design was important, too, it had a really New York vibe to it. It was a magical place. And the fashion. All the girls dressed down, there were a lot of dungarees, baggy t-shirts and baggy jeans. It was very sweaty in there. People would wear bumbags too.

There's a convergence of a few things as to why it worked in Manchester. Manchester had a great music scene that was dominated by Factory Records, the drugs helped, and northerners tend to like faster music than southerners.

The two or three years that I spent playing there changed my life forever. From there, my outlook became very international. I was on the guest circuit internationally and UK wide, so personally that changes your whole outlook. It was revolutionary. It only takes one experience of ecstasy to loosen up and you saw that happening first hand.

The club is really important to me, it's a family for a lot of us.

Above // Dancers at the club. The man on the left is wearing a 'Hallucienda' t-shirt, based on the night that opened in 1989 and ran on a Monday. The t-shirt became one of the club's best sellers.

HEATRE
JOIN OUR
MAILING

Opposite (top) // Tony Wilson with Happy Mondays manager, Nathan McGough.

Below // Suzanne Jackson and James Masters, Head of Media for the Haçienda.**Suzanne** remembers: “There is no greater journey than James’ jouirney with the Haçienda, his second family.”

Left (above and below) **//** Club-goer Jon Harris and friends, circa 1990.

The
United States
of the
Haçienda

Fac 51
Manchester
England
1990

Trance American Tour

DJ's Mike Pickering, Paul Oakenfold, Graeme Park, Dave Haslam

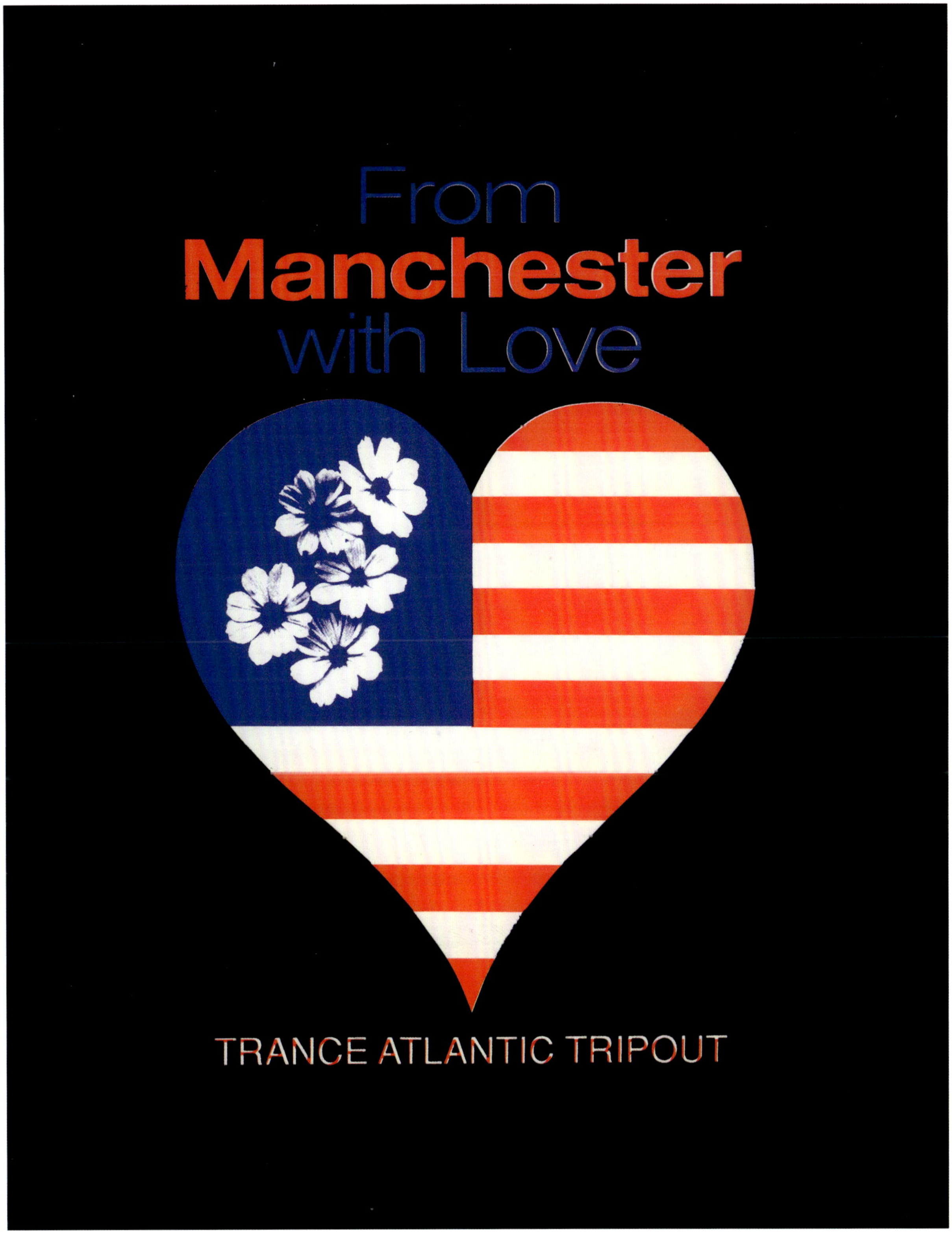

Opposite and above // The United States of the Haçienda saw the club take DJs Mike Pickering, Paul Oakenfold, Graeme Park and Dave Haslam on a tour of the US, covering Miami, Dallas, Boston, Chicago and New York among other destinations. **Paul Cons**: "We ended up in New York, playing at the Sound Factory. I'd had Delight pestering me for months to book them, so I finally relented, though I didn't really have a clue who they were. By the time we got to New York, thousands of people were queuing just to see them – they had no idea what the Haçienda even was."

K-Klass are house music pioneers who first met at the Haçienda in 1988. Bobbi Depasois, Russ Morgan and Paul Roberts are all members of the group.

Russ: I went to the Haçienda for the first time in 1984 and it was empty. We'd come on a coach, there was about 40 or 50 of us and when we went inside, we doubled the amount of people in there.

It wasn't until '88 when I went back that the space had completely changed, that's when I bumped into Paul. My friend had said "if you like house music you should go on a Friday night", so I went back and I was blown away, it absolutely changed my life.

Paul: I'd seen New Order a few times there and I was a big fanboy at the time, so that was my early experience of the club. In '88 someone had told me about what was going on there, so I went back and it was like night and day compared to what I'd seen before. The atmosphere, the intensity, the togetherness, it was like one big family.

At the time we really did think that we were changing the world. House music was a hotbed in Manchester, and when ecstasy and dance music came together everything exploded – it was like a really big secret that you didn't want too many people to know about.

Russ: We were that committed to going that one night Paul and I drove there in the snow – you couldn't see the white lines on the motorway it was that bad. But we had to go, we had to be there.

Paul: I'd go on my own sometimes and you'd always buddy up with a group of people. One week you'd find yourself in Stoke afterwards, the other you'd be sat in someone's house in Huddersfield.

I'd leave the club with no money left a lot of the time, and end up thumbing it back to Chester. It really was the be-all and end-all of everything, no matter what, your whole week and your whole world revolved around going there.

Bobbi: Music in Manchester is such a big deal. When we started going out people were so inspired, and we just wanted to make our own music.

Paul: I've always been blown away by people's enthusiasm for music in Manchester. In Chester, where I'm from, the clubs were just horrible, violent places.

Russ: People dug deep in the Manchester community, and you found music that you'd never normally come across.

Paul: When the house music scene kicked off I used to have a copper cable right the way around the top of my bedroom and connected into my stereo so that I could pick up Stu Allan's show in Manchester. I'd write down the names of all the tracks then get the train into Manchester the next day to go to Eastern Bloc and buy them all.

When people go out now, 90 per cent of the time they want familiarity. We were actively going out of our way to seek out things that we had never heard before.

There was a big West Indian community in Manchester and there had also been the Northern Soul scene, so everything was already in place for the Haçienda to take off.

Our creative process was massively influenced by what we were experiencing there. The club brought us altogether. Our first release came about after a night in the club, we'd bumped into a band from Wrexham there called Interstate, who we had seen performing with 808 State and we loved their sound. They sounded exactly like what we had been hearing at the club. They invited us to go back to their house in Wrexham and they had a tiny little box room with a Roland TR-909, and as soon as they hit the kick drum we were like "wow, that's exactly what we're looking for".

It was a real DIY attitude, it was the first time since punk that you could make a record for next to nothing. We pressed that first EP onto chrome cassettes and took it to Eastern Bloc – we didn't even have a name for the band or anything at that point.

Russ: We were the most unmusical people in the world, we didn't know how to play a chord or anything right up to when we released

'Rhythm is a Mystery'. The only reason we started the band in the first place was to get a track played in the Haçienda.

Paul: Someone said to us that 'Rhythm Is a Mystery' was going down really well in the club, so we went down on the next Saturday that we had off. I still remember it to this day, we were stood on the balcony looking down on the dancefloor just before midnight and there was a ripple of appreciation when the track kicked in. The place went up and we were all just stood there with our jaws on the floor.

Russ: To be played in that club was all we ever wanted, we didn't even have a follow up to 'Rhythm Is a Mystery'!

Paul: There was a wave of bands around at that time that one day would be doing a normal job or be unemployed, and then the next they'd be on *Top of the Pops* out of nowhere.

From meeting Bobbi to the management we had, none of it would have happened if it wasn't for the club. Everything in the early days centred around it.

Bobbi: I was born in Moss Side and there was so much going on there musically. You were constantly out dancing, seven nights a week.

Paul: So many lifelong relationships were formed in that club – me and Bobbi are married, for one! You were mixing with people from different parts of the country and different walks of life, people that you wouldn't cross paths with on a day-to-day basis. Everyone had one endgame and that was to go and dance to some fantastic music.

Bobbi: We were all just on a rave wave!

Paul: The whole scene was endearing and it has stuck with people for a lifetime.

The fashion in the club used to change on a fortnightly basis. There'd be the dayglo acid house smileys but by winter people would be stood on the stage in fishermen's jumpers and dungarees.

Russ: I'd wear brands like Kickers, Clarks' Wallabees and Converse. Then you'd start wearing trainers with jeans, anything loose fit was a good choice because you would come out of there absolutely soaking.

Paul: The whole thing was a massive counterculture, we were completely rebelling against everything that a traditional nightclub was. That's what made it so special. The love for the Haçienda is on another level.

> The whole thing was a massive counterculture, we were completely rebelling against everything that a traditional nightclub was. That's what made it so special. The love for the Haçienda is on another level.

Paul Roberts

Luke Unabomber is a DJ and promoter who was at the heart of Manchester and Sheffield's rave scenes.

I was living in Sheffield and first came over to the club in '85/'86. I eventually moved to Manchester permanently and would often go to Nude at the club on a Friday night, which was predominantly house music, but before acid house. It was a 70 per cent Black crowd, lots of jazz dancers, it was a relatively small scene at that time. I was a convert from very early on.

Before acid house and ecstasy, the club was a very different place, it had so many different moments and waves, but for me that was it and I went to the club throughout them all for the next six years.

It was a temple in some ways, just purely the visual side of it. Most clubs were either basements, dark dives – which I love – or they were quite tacky commercial clubs where the music was bad and people danced around handbags.

The Haçienda was a combination of underground music and this huge brutalist industrial space, it was like nothing I'd ever seen before.

I guess serendipity, creativity and explosions of culture, art and music is why it worked in Manchester. I believe that at some point things come together with synergy at the right time at the right place, whether it's Berlin in the '90s or acid house. I think the club could have happened anywhere, but it happened in Manchester because of a huge passion for music in a big, very mixed and diverse city.

People were dancing to this music that was made on machines that sounded like the shock of the new and before any drugs turned up it was completely uniting so many people.

The North was a fucking brutal place in the early '80s and I think the club just caught a moment. Who knows why these things happen, they never last and then they reappear again somewhere else. I've seen it happen time and time again – it's just infinite creativity.

It was a blue-collar working-class movement, its origins are in Black queer music from the States. There was a diversity and inclusivity that I'd never seen before. Whoever you were did not matter – I've never seen such an explosive thing. There was a real togetherness, and no one gave a fuck who you were. That unity of the late-night disenfranchised was quite remarkable.

There was a real warmth and a love that you didn't get anywhere else. It felt like a church. It was the shock of the new if you compare what went before it.

Whether you're spiritual or not you were definitely taken somewhere else. I still believe 40 years on that it was something beyond the hedonism and nihilism of just taking drugs. When things aren't great in life music becomes a really important thing. It's undeniable that music to British youth in the '80s was incomparable to anywhere else.

Football culture played a massive part in the fashion at the club. People were going around Europe in the '80s and coming back from Ibiza between '84 and '86 in strange clothes, baggy clothes and ponchos before acid house was even a thing. The movement was started by the Manchester, Sheffield, Northern and London hoodlums who travelled around Europe robbing shops.

There was also a lot more of a dressed-down look in Manchester, people would wear Ralph Lauren or baggy clothes and had either short hair or longer styles, but football was a huge influence on all of that.

I met Lucy [Scher] in '88 and she was living in a lesbian commune in Hulme, which was a huge council estate that was quite lawless. Nobody paid rent and the council allowed it to happen because they knew it was going to be knocked down. Lucy and her crew ran a lesbian fruit and veg shop. I just loved the liberation of it.

Things were changing at the time of Flesh. There was alpha politics, cocaine was coming in, which brought with it aggression, and Flesh was an ecosystem that was protected from that, it felt like a very pure, liberated place. There was a real sense of innocence and idealism in those days where it didn't matter.

Above // DJ Sasha performing at the club.

♥ from Manchester with love

Opposite // DJ, record producer and influential figure in the acid house movement, Andrew Weatherall.

Left // The acid house scene was a rebirth for the club, a period when it began to become a destination for those all over the country and even Europe.

'89 to '91 was the golden period. Madchester was in full flow – this ridiculous mash-up of baggy bacchanalia, coupled with a fervour on the dancefloor, which was breathtaking in the extreme.

Graeme Park

Opposite // Chaotic scenes towards the end of the club's 8th birthday party in 1990.

Above // Paul Cons: "Hot was all about summer. Palm trees, beach balls, so much smoke you couldn't see where you were. And it was absolutely packed every week."

Kevin Cummins is a photographer. He was chief photographer at the *NME* for over ten years.

I first went to the Haçienda before it opened. Tony got me down to have a look and encourage me to take some pictures, but I didn't think there was much point until they'd finished building it, so I waited until the opening night instead. That was fairly disastrous, like a lot of early evenings there, but the club looked great.

When it opened it was hugely different to anything else in Manchester. It felt new. A lot of Manchester venues were dingy cellar bars. The Haçienda looked good with the lights on – nowhere else did. It wasn't that people were crying out for something new, but we'd been to a few clubs in New York and thought that same approach would work in Manchester. We were arrogant enough to think that Manchester was same as New York, forgetting that Andy Warhol and Liza Minnelli wouldn't turn up on our first night. The only celebrity we had was Martin Fry, because he was friends with Mike Pickering.

In the early days it felt like a social club for people who worked at Factory Records. It was easy for me, as my studio was less than a mile away. I'd quite often photograph bands there during the week because the stage was painted black and there was natural light coming in. I'd just ask Mike or Howard Jones and they'd let me in. It became my unofficial studio.

I met Ian Griffiths when I was doing a piece for *The Face* on New Romantics. I went to Pips and Placemate – two Manchester clubs – to take some shots and saw Ian dressed as Henry VIII. I got chatting to him and he said he made all his own stuff. There was no-one else quite like that in Manchester, so I told him to come down to the studio with a few of his outfits so we could take some portraits. They didn't end up using them in *The Face*, they wanted the club shots instead. There was quite a patronising attitude at the magazine then to anywhere outside of London. They thought everyone up north made their own clothes anyway.

If gigs at the club were good it was because of the atmosphere and the occasion. Technically, I thought it was a terrible place to see bands live, the sound seemed to get swallowed up beneath the stage. So I wouldn't say gigs there really deserve to be listened back to, they were very much of the moment. It was chaos when The Smiths played, and The Birthday Party were great. Einsturzende Neubauten tried to chainsaw through one of the pillars, which didn't go down so well. I thought Madonna was fun. She came along after about eight of us saw her perform on the roof of Danceteria in New York in July '83 and Rob Gretton asked her if she fancied coming over and playing a gig. Then *The Tube* got involved and wanted to film it and it all got taken a bit out of his hands.

It could have closed at any time in the early years. But when the Haçienda understood its worth and became a superclub, when people started travelling from all over the world to go there, that's when it came into its own and became a great club. The acid house scene was massive, and they didn't need bands for that. I'd moved to London a few years prior, but we'd sometimes organise a coach trip from the *NME* offices to go up on a Friday night, stay until 4am and then come back the next morning.

There were a few of us at the *NME* at that time who were really into the Haçienda and the Manchester scene, and we helped perhaps to elevate it beyond its own importance. Between 1988 and 1991 we put Manchester acts on about a third of our covers. There were enough of us championing the city to be able to do that. It's self-generating in a way. You'll have bands influenced by Buzzcocks, the Smiths, Happy Mondays, the Stone Roses, then Oasis – there's a great lineage in Manchester. And there were people there to document it, which helped enormously. There were good scenes in other cities, but we didn't give a toss.

When I took photographs at the club I tried to capture a sense of the atmosphere and show how packed it was with 1,500 people together in a steamy room. I shot the nights I liked the most, so you were totally immersed in what was going on. It's not at all like shooting a band, I didn't try to get many individual portraits. I might pick out one person in a crowd as a focal point and then the rest of the scene would look after itself.

There are two photographs that I really feel encapsulate the club. The first is a silhouette, a crowd of people with their hands in the air. The second is one I took of a couple of lads at the end of a night, walking away from a scene of absolute carnage. It looks like something from *Apocalypse Now*.

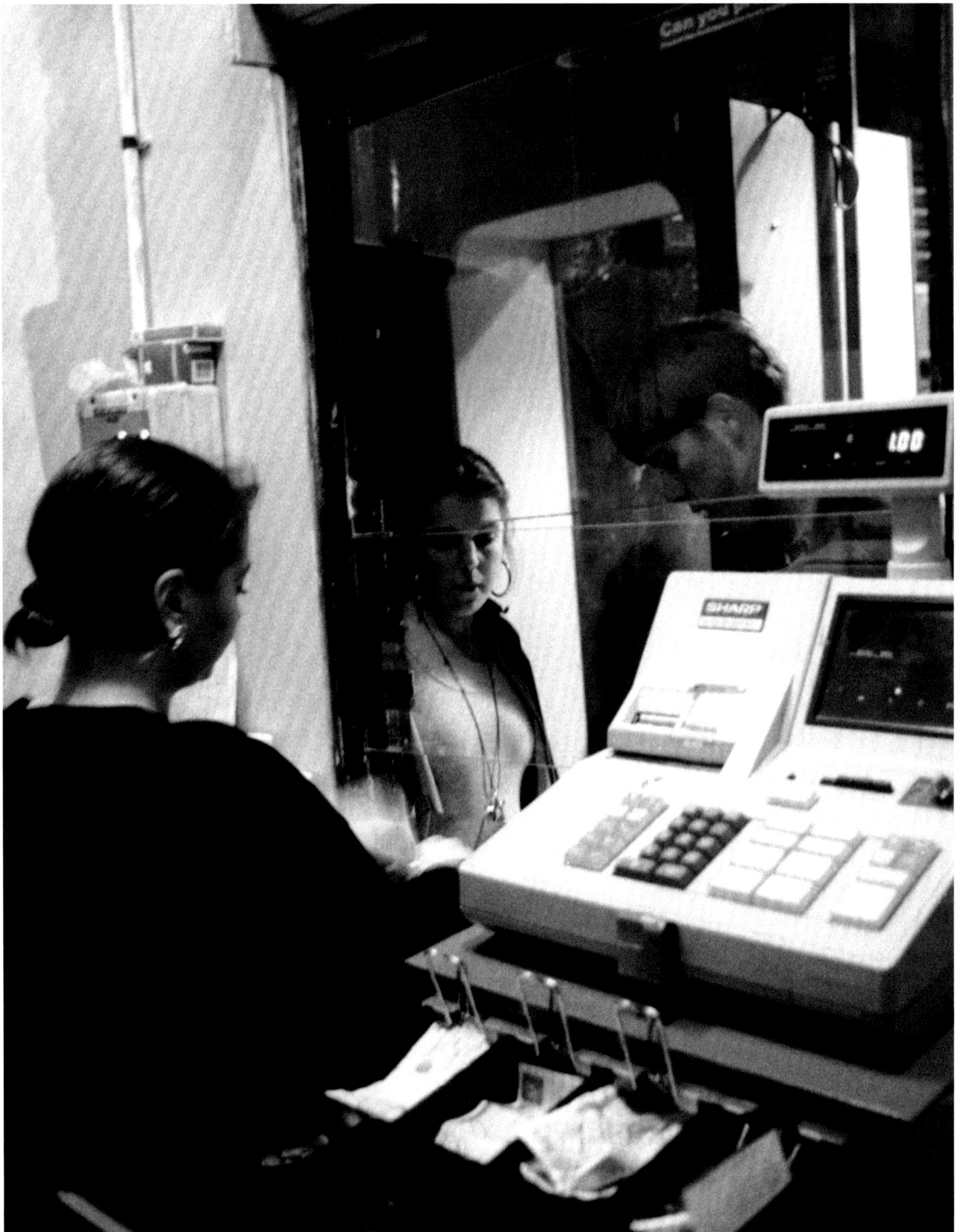
SHARP

Opposite and above // The queue and front desk at the club. In the late '80s and early '90s, as large groups began to descend on the club by the coachload, the queue to get in became a destination in its own right.

Bez Is a member of the Happy Mondays and a legendary figure of the Manchester music scene.

For me, the Haçienda was that moment in my life where things changed forever. If it wasn't for that club, I wouldn't be the man I am stood in front of you today. It shaped me.

It put me on the straight and narrow and completely changed my life. I'm so grateful to Factory Records, the Haçienda, and that whole journey I went on from the moment I stepped foot in the club. We used to have big dreams and it helped us realise them. I've never looked back and the whole experience changed me forever.

We knew it was a magical place straightaway. Back in the day you'd go to clubs, and everyone was dressed up in shirts and fancy clothes – a bit up themselves. But when we walked into that club, it was like walking into heaven. You could do whatever you wanted in there – smoke weed, dress however you liked – and we just thought to ourselves, "fucking hell, this is what freedom feels like".

Opposite // Bez amongst the revellers on the dancefloor.

SONY
VOID
RoXY
SERGIO MENDES
GET DOWN RECORDS
EDWARD GET DOWN
CATCH THE BEAT
DOUBLE TROUBLE
THE REBEL MC

The two or three years that I spent playing there changed my life forever… It was revolutionary… The club is really important to me, it's a family for a lot of us.

Jon Dasilva

Opposite // DJ Jon Dasilva.

FAC51
SECURITY

STELLA
ARTOIS

Rowetta is a singer, known for her work with the Happy Mondays and solo career.

One of the first times I remember being in the Haçienda was when I met Bez. I'd been playing a gig at The Ritz and he came down to the front of the stage, then we bumped into each other later on in the Haç. I was wearing a pair of denim cut-off shorts with really long, dangly frayed bits and Bez thought they were my pubes!

I usually dressed like a punk back then, I wore a lot of leather. From 1989 onwards I would sit with the lads [Happy Mondays] and I didn't go and dance on the dancefloor really, I'd spend a lot of time sat in the corner and would only move to go and ask the DJ for a tune. I was treated differently when I joined the Mondays because I was the only well-known girl that went in, we'd sometimes come straight off the tour bus and people would say "it must be great being you" and it was amazing.

I used to hear my voice a lot in the club, I didn't know that you could sample people back then. I remember going up to the DJ and saying, "What's this tune? That's my voice on it!" it was a surreal but incredible moment.

The legacy lives on in the music and the DJs that came out of the club. Everyone was smiling and so warm and loving.

'You've Got the Love' by Candi Staton defines the Haçienda for me, I just remember hearing that in the club and never wanting it to end.

Opposite // Rowetta performs with Bez and Shaun Ryder as the Happy Mondays in 1991.

Fac 51 **The Haçien**

As you may already know, **the Grea** be applying to revoke the **Haçienda** **17th of May.**

We will of course be rigorously defer

Despite our major efforts in recent m removing the use of **illegal drugs** in **not,** repeat, **NOT,** buy, or take drugs

The prime role of your club is a place only way it can continue in this way is

It's our club – and it's your club – we' to be fighting with us.

PLEASE MAKE SURE EVERYON MESSAGE IS. *Let's rock* – **legally.**

Directors: Anthony Wilson, Alan Erasmus, Rob
Management: Paul Mason, Paul Cons, Leroy
Dj's: Mike Pickering, Graeme Park, John daS

A MESSAGE TO ALL OUR CUSTOMERS:

lanchester Police have told us that they will
ense at the next magistrates meeting on the

the action with all our energy.

s, the police feel we must do even more about
the Haçienda – this is where you come in – **do**
club – and do not bring drugs onto the premises.

ance to the most important music of the day; the
e complete elimination of controlled substances.

ng to **fight** to keep it alive and we expect you

IDERSTANDS HOW IMPORTANT THIS

n, Bernard Sumner, Peter Hook, Steve Morris, Gillian Gilbert.
dson.
ick Arrojo, Dave Haslam.

1991-

1993

The concept of gay liberation sounds as culturally antiquated as other last-century causes, like burning your bra or banning the bomb. But by the early 1990s, gay people had had enough. Liberation, as the Pet Shop Boys would remind us, was all about finding real love, and the freedom that comes with acceptance.

The prevailing attitudes and damning rhetoric of the previous decade was enough to make anyone run to the hills. AIDS had decimated the gay community, and society blamed innocent young men for a disease that would show no mercy.

But 1991 was one of those gateway years when barriers were toppling quicker than people could put them up. Acid house, for all its intoxicated idealism, had taught people to be more accepting. Serotonin levels may have been artificially spiked, but the resultant effect was a beautiful thing to behold. In clubs up and down the country, straights and gays, breeders and bummers, plus all manner of "Betty Bothways" came together. The Haçienda proved to be the perfect collision point.

This was a period of flux at the Haçienda. The club had been besieged with issues in recent years, and as its popularity rose, problems duly followed. When drugs filtered into the club, so did the gangsters, eager to capitalise on this booming night-time economy. In a remarkably canny move, Paul Cons proposed a once-a-month mid-week venture, Flesh, which began a successful two-year reign in the autumn of 1991. This – for the most part – would be a gay-only affair, therefore eliminating the rougher elements intent on soiling the club's reputation.

Cons, together with fellow promoter Lucy Scher, had form, putting on gay events in the city with increasing success. They felt confident they could fill the Haçienda's cavernous space, and, inspired by his Factory-funded trips to New York, Cons set out to dazzle. On the main floor, DJ Tim Lennox spun the kind of podium-straddling house music that set the place on fire. Downstairs, in The Gay Traitor Bar, with a portrait of disgraced spy Anthony Blunt hanging on the wall, fierce ruling queens Kath McDermott and DJ Paulette battled condensation and overflowing toilets while funking it up in royal style.

"Flesh was a seminal night for many reasons," says Paulette. "You can't undersell how important it was. Before Flesh happened, there were gay nights in Manchester, but there wasn't a night that brought everybody together. Before that, you had the art set, the lesbians, the gay guys, the leather guys, but everyone went to their own space, they didn't mix, and the scene was really fractured. What Flesh did was put gayness, and young gayness, out there openly, and in the biggest club in Manchester. It was like: we're here, get used to it. We're not going to hide away, we're not gonna feel like we're dirty, or what we have is catching. We're going to embrace life and party. We're going to dress up in our finery and be who we want to be."

There were other nights at the Haçienda in 1991, but Flesh is the one that people remember. This was a night to see and be seen. "It didn't copy what had come before it," says Paulette. "It wasn't baggy, or curtain hair-dos. I mean, it did have an element of that, but there was so much else going on in there. And it transcended the drugs and crime element because it kept them out. You're going to have a lot less trouble in a gay club than in a straight club, and that's why they did it, to keep the gangs at bay."

Out and proud DJ Kath McDermott is in thrall to these near-mythical monthly parties. "I think prior to Flesh, a lot of people thought the Haçienda was coming to a bit of a close, that it had had its moment. Flesh created renewed energy for those final years, not only for queer people but for straight people too that

05

had been Haçienda regulars but didn't go to the other nights anymore because they'd ended up being a bit edgy. People came to Flesh because it was fun and easy and they didn't feel threatened."

The very fact the Haçienda was built around the premise of world-beating gay clubs like New York's Paradise Garage makes this happy union all the more prescient. "Can you imagine seeing the Haçienda full of gay people?" she says. "Everyone had been talking about it for years, so to see that happen was just an amazing moment. Whether they were straight or gay, people were desperate to get in. Going to gay clubs suddenly turned into a cool thing to do. And the fact that the best gay club in the country was outside London was a real first. It kick-started Gaychester. Up until that point, Manchester had punched above its weight, but it wasn't an international gay city. After Flesh, it really started building in that direction."

For the butch dykes, muscle Marys and baby gays of the time, it was all too much. Future *Coronation Street* actor Anthony Crank readily admits that, for his teenage self, Flesh was an overwhelming experience. "I was obsessed with the Haçienda from a very early age," he smiles. "It was the subject I wrote about for my GSCE English exam! I was also obsessed with Jason Orange from Take That. I used to see him at Flesh with Paula Yates, and I think Gianni Versace was in there with him one time too. Chris Evans, Naomi Campbell, Leigh Bowery, all these amazing people passed through Flesh. When Kinky Gerlinky came up from London, Leigh Bowery chased me all around the club, with that weird wooden leg. That's an image you never forget."

"Oh God, that was the night Leigh 'gave birth' on stage," says McDermott. "Just another 'happening' at Flesh, but one that will go down in history."

"One of my abiding memories is coming down the stairs to The Gay Traitor," remembers photographer and 'Flesh Face' Lee Baxter. "You'd see Paulette, DJing in her silver bikini top, and you were like, Oh, right, everything's fitting into place now. The party has started."

"That's hilarious," laughs Paulette. "The fact is, we had to make everything from scratch. For a lot of us back then, nothing was off the peg."

Naturally, and as is ever the case in clubland, fashion was elemental. Manchester had always fostered its own unique take on style, but by now was utterly absorbed in the cult of the designer. Oscar Hervia OBE, a Chilean emigré, who, in the late 70s, had escaped the dictatorship of Pinochet, was now the proprietor of his own eponymous store. Hervia, the leading purveyor of club couture for the Mancunian sartorialist, stocked covetable labels such as Y3, Comme des Garçons and Vivienne Westwood. The savvy South American was in high demand. "Westwood was really popular with that kind of crowd," he recalls. "We sold so many Orb pendants, it was unbelievable. And they were so heavy. They'd be bouncing up and down on people's necks, which would be bright red by the end of the night."

Famously, but with little fanfare, the great designer herself visited the club one memorable night. "When Vivienne arrived, everybody was pushed outside on the pavement to let her in," says Hervia, by then the official franchisee for the brand. "It was quite a violent time, so I was worried. But they ushered us through the centre of the club and took us underneath the stage. We had a few drinks down there with some of the staff. What was her tipple? She said she quite liked whiskey, so Ang Matthews brought in a whole bottle and put it in front of her, like an offering. I'm not sure Vivienne was a nightclub person but she was impressed by the Haçienda and all its madness, It was a memorable evening. As they all were at Flesh."

Above // Scenes behind the scenes at the club, including at Hicks bar, which continued a theme established by The Gay Traitor by taking its name from that of a Soviet double agent.

Above // Signs of real life: snapshots of days and nights at the club, provided by former staff and the club's greatest asset: the clubbers.

O ADMITTANCE
POSITIVA

FAC 51
THE HACIENDA

Jingle Bells,
Jingle Bells,
Jingle all the way,
Oh what fun it is to be,
Down at the Hacienda at Christmas.
("It doesn't rhyme but who cares")

Above and following pages // The club frequently threw themed nights, but this fancy-dress Christmas party was for Haçienda staff only.

You could walk into the Haçienda and, even if none of your mates were there, you could sit with the bar staff – it had a real community feel... I never socialised anywhere else.

Ang Matthews

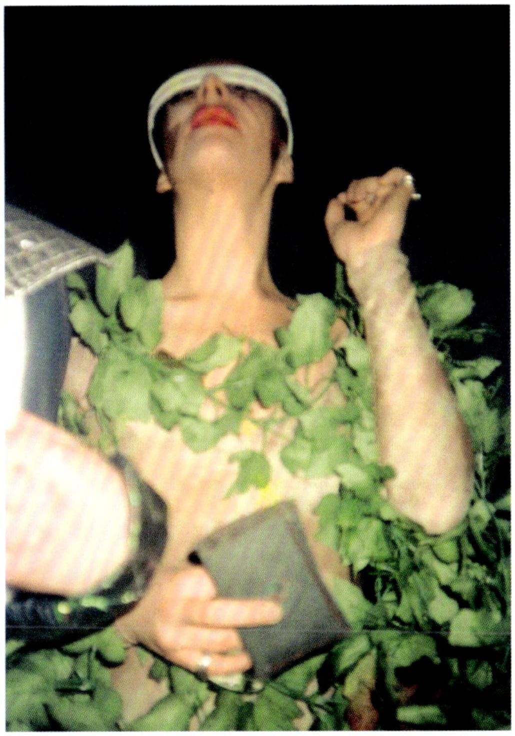
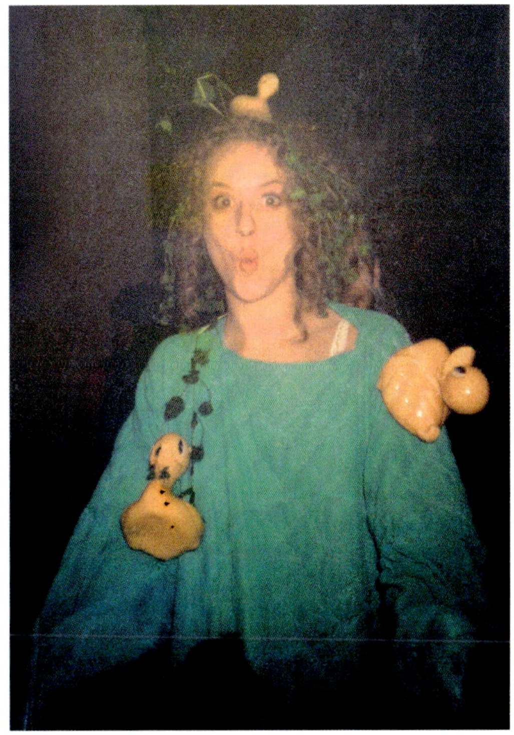

oXY

Right and opposite // Further scenes and adventures at the Haç.

Previous page // Happy Mondays perform at the club.

Left // Pet Shop Boys play the club's 10th birthday celebrations in May 1992. The band performed in front of a backdrop of films created by artist and film-maker Derek Jarman, who also introduced them ahead of their performance. Some of the proceeds from the night were donated to the Village Charity, a gay charity in Manchester.

Ronika and Jemima were door hosts and dancers at the night Flesh.

Jemima: We were living in Hulme and travelling a lot at the end of the '80s/early '90s. When we would get back to Manchester, we'd spend all of our time making outfits to go clubbing in. We would live a really unhealthy lifestyle for a few months and then think, shit, we need to get fit again, so we'd get back on our bikes for a month or so before doing it all again.

Ronika: We'd just left Greenham Common. We moved to Manchester because we had decided that it was brilliant being political but actually, we just really wanted to be disco bunnies full time. The Haçienda and Flesh was the place to do just that.

The first night we went to was Lucy Scher's Lesbian Summer of Love. We weren't living in Manchester at that time, so we travelled over with nowhere to stay and no way of getting home, but we got taken in by a very friendly lesbian.

What attracted me to the club was that it was just full of really fabulous lesbians who were all dressed amazingly. We automatically wanted to live there.

Jemima: Coming from Greenham Common, which is very political and right on, it felt extremely liberating.

Ronika: It all felt very sexy. We both ended up working for Suzanne in the kitchen as her cycle couriers, delivering sandwiches and all sorts of things around Manchester.

Lucy had seen us out a lot dancing and me and Jemima would often wear the same outfits or a theme. We both had really long dreadlocks and we got dressed up, but at that time dykes didn't really get dressed up in that way. We wore dresses and that wasn't really the done thing if you were lesbian back then, so we really stood out. We were really alternative. We'd wear a tutu with suspenders and huge boots to the club.

We would go to jumble sales or charity shops or find old curtains to make our outfits from. We'd spend a whole month making really elaborate stuff for Flesh. It was a massively important thing.

Jemima: We'd spend all day getting ready for it. It's nuts that it was on a Wednesday night.

Ronika: One of the funniest outfits we designed was for a beach-themed night at Flesh. We wore Y-fronts and pinned hundreds of safety pins to the front, as well as maternity bras with zips in and these amazing straw hats that were from Iran. We were onstage dancing that night, which was our original job before we got on the door.

For us, Flesh was like a family. There was us, loads of other dancers, Paulette and Kath would be DJing – all of our friends were there. Our job was to get everybody dancing.

There was always something mad going on. I remember a piercer being there one night and I went up to him before it started and said, "I'm going to come over later and I want my navel pierced, I'm going to be off my face but I'm telling you now that I definitely want it."

There was porn sometimes. I remember Lucy [Scher] sending me to buy loads of magazines one night. We used to do leafleting for Flesh as well. I remember getting thrown out of Paradise Factory once for leafleting in there.

Jemima: Flesh wasn't in an underground club somewhere, it was really exposed. Everybody wanted to go. It was the place to be. It felt like it was lifted and celebrated, unlike other queer clubs we had been in before.

Ronika: It wasn't a lesbian thing at all to be wild and sexy, but that's exactly what you were at Flesh.

It was like having Pride once a month. It was just full of fabulous people and they would come from all over the country to experience it at the Haçienda.

Jemima: It wasn't as accepted to be queer in those days, it was all very underground, so we all had our friend families. We became closer than you would normally become in friendship groups because we had to be so careful. That's what forged such strong bonds.

Ronika: We knew that we were part of something amazing. We had come from these grubby little lesbian clubs and suddenly we were part of this incredible thing where everybody was just really fucking fabulous.

That space made us feel totally fearless, we felt like we ruled the world. When we were working on the door, straight people used to try to convince us that they were gay so that we could let them in and it was the first time that gay people were able to say "nope, not tonight. This is for us, not for you" and that felt good.

We felt totally invincible, gorgeous, powerful and really proud to be queer. I was studying Arabic at university at the time, and I used to just keep my head down. After going to Flesh I'd proudly wear my "queer as fuck" t-shirt; I didn't care what people thought about me because we completely ruled that night. It was next level confidence.

We weren't just accepted at Flesh, people wanted to be us. We found our place and our tribe and nothing makes you feel more powerful than that.

I think the fact that Flesh was at the Haçienda was so important. It couldn't have been anywhere else. It was so happening there, so the fact that a big queer night was there too just brought it all together.

Right // Ronika and Jemima.

Last Wednesday of eve
Serious pleasure fo
FL
Fac 51 The Haçienda,

month

ykes and Queers

SH

nchester. 061) 236 5051

Above // **Michelle Kelly** (centre) remembers: "With my friends Lucy (left) and Candy (right). I will always remember the time Candy sprayed her bra and hot pants with gold car spray, then off we all went to Flesh – where it was totally acceptable to be wearing just a bra, or no bra, in Lucy's case."

Opposite // Clubber **Paula Bowden** remembers: "My brother Richard ran Cheerleaders, the bar next door, so we were often taken round and let through without having to pay – though I loved the queue, it was part of the night. I especially loved Flesh, the questions they asked at the door to check if you were gay."

Left and opposite // Manchester-based fashion designer Consalvo Pellecchia was part of the local creative scene that encompassed the club, with his clothes even modelled by DJ Paulette (opposite, top left and bottom right). **Consalvo** remembers: "I feel very lucky to have grown up in that era. It was definitely a brilliant time to be an independent designer and manufacturer. Seeing women wearing my designs at the Haçienda was always special and gave me a great buzz. It meant I'd got it right – in terms of the style, cut, fabric and, most of all, the vibe."

NO DRINKS
ON FLOOR

My memories of reaching the final of the Haçienda's karaoke competition are hazy, as indeed all memories should be of those wonderful, halcyonic evenings of yore. It was a brilliant evening that put me on the route to dedicating my whole life to performance.

David Hoyle

Opposite // Divine David (otherwise known as performing artist David Hoyle and no stranger to the Haçienda's stage) was crowned winner of the Miss Flesh beauty pageant.

In Conversation

Paul Cons ran the club's legendary night, Flesh.

Michelle Kelly is a fashion stylist who has worked with Rihanna, Taylor Swift and Nelly Furtado and whose work has appeared in *Vogue*, *Tatler* and *GQ*.

Paul Flynn is a journalist whose work has appeared in *LOVE*, *Fantastic Man* and *i-D*. He is author of the book *Good As You: From Prejudice to Pride – 30 Years of Gay Britain*.

Paul Cons: I was walking down King Street one afternoon and a Vidal Sassoon hairdresser came out and asked if they could cut my hair. I said yes and I ended up at a Vidal Sassoon show at the Haçienda as a model – that was my introduction to the club.

I got a job as a promotions assistant, so I used to give out flyers for events, and that led to me becoming the promotions manager. It was the coolest and most exciting space in Manchester at that time. There was nothing else quite like it.

Michelle: I was still at school when I first went – we were absolutely obsessed with it. When I first went, my friend rang up Paul [Cons] and said that we worked in the wardrobe department at Granada Studios so could we get on the guest list – and he said yeah! We were so excited; we couldn't believe it.

That was it then, though, I had caught the bug. I met so many friends there, all really important people that I still know now.

Paul Flynn: I was at school in Wythenshawe and I had an older brother and sister who had been. The draw for me was that the weirdos went there. The first time I went I was 15 and I took my brother's driving licence.

Walking into the place for the first time was as alien to me as walking on a crater on the moon. It felt like you were in outer space. There was something amazingly scary about it all and that was what drew you back. We learned how to be cool at the Haçienda.

It changed everything overnight. I used to read *The Face* and *i-D* magazine and you'd see the club all over the pages, but it was so much bigger than that. The mythology that surrounded it was so entrenched and deep, it made you look at the world in a whole new way. It was an elixir of youth. All your energy just went in a really positive direction.

You can't underestimate it. Even if people didn't go there or didn't know what it was there was always a story about it. You half knew what went on behind the doors before you got in but then once you arrived it completely flipped. Seeing the reality of it was different, you felt like you had earned your place there.

Michelle: I felt like I was in the inner sanctum. Everybody in there was so glamorous and fabulous and I knew that these were my people.

I used to stay up until 5 in the morning and I was just high on life and happy to be there. I met so many amazing people.

Paul Cons: The birth of Flesh stemmed from unfinished business that I had with my club night Gay Monday. The combination of the drugs and the music at the Haçienda made it the obvious place to give it another go, and my friend Lucy Scher had just done the Lesbian Summer of Love in the club. She managed to get about 1,000 lesbians and that's what made me realise that Flesh could actually be possible. This was around the time that the club had to shut because of the gang issues, but I met with Tony [Wilson] and said to him that when we reopen, I think one way of not having any gang trouble is to do a big gay night.

The club had gone a bit sleazy and a bit rough, so a really great glamorous gay night was exactly what it needed. Tony [Wilson] paid for me to go to New York at the end of the '80s, so I caught the tail end of the New York club scene of that era and it really inspired Flesh.

We had a lot of people that would come to Flesh with no clothes on and a lot that were very scantily dressed.

Ecstasy is the catalyst here – that drug is what fuelled the whole thing.

Paul Flynn: It all exploded at the same time, the music and the drug. The '80s was so universally terrible that you almost felt like you had earned the party at the end.

Michelle: Flesh was a pioneer of gay culture.

Paul Cons: The genius of the Haçienda was that it was in a city big enough to have lots of scenes, but small enough for you to just have one club where they could all go.

Michelle: It was always about what you were going to wear to Flesh and there'd usually be a theme. We'd often go to the wardrobe department of the BBC or hire some massive costumes – I remember going as a Christmas fairy once.

Paul Flynn: Paul took the weight of it on his shoulders, if you'd left that up to a Mancunian, God knows what mess we would've been in.

Michelle: Even if you weren't into fetish gear, you would buy and wear it specifically for those Wednesday nights at Flesh.

Paul Cons: People took the Flesh thing quite literally and would turn up wearing next to nothing. There were a lot of angel wings at Flesh, too, which I think was carried over from the New York scene.

Paul Flynn: Another minority is nightclub people, and they're always the best kind of people.

Paul Cons: It was a completely formative time and the friendships that we all made, they've lasted.

Paul Flynn: I think the thing with a nightclub is that it's segregated on the grounds of taste, but then if you have taste and sexuality together, that's quite a potent mix.

I think clubbing is much more formative than school. Even though you were common as muck, it gave you a layer of sophistication and confidence.

Opposite and above // Dancers at Flesh, performing under the stage name Aphrodisiac. This photograph was used on a flyer promoting the night.

Above left // Joanne Collin remembers: "I started going to the Haçienda in 1991 and was there with friends most weekends. In March 1993 we went to a 'Haçienda meets Ministry of Sound' event in London, it was an amazing night and I met a guy there, who I met up with again at the Haç three weeks later. We've been together ever since, were married in 1998 and have two children. The Haçienda was a massive part of our lives."

Above right // Elton Jackson remembers: "At the opening night of Shiva, my 'club kids' friends Lee Baxter and Tim decided to dress appropriately. Tim wore about twenty metres of brown ribbed fabric wrapped around himself, which kept falling off to reveal him in just pants and trainers underneath. We were the first people on the dance floor and caused quite a stir. The Haç was my Mecca. It allowed me to be me, even against all the odds. So many people from differing backgrounds coming together, dancing. It was like a protest."

Opposite // From an April 1992 Kinky Gerlinky night, held as part of Flesh at the Haçienda.

Left // Kath McDermott in the main room. **Kath:** "Most of my friends I met on the dancefloor at the Haçienda… It's in our blood. It's in every club and every DJ that ever went there. It was life changing for me."

Opposite // DJ Paulette in The Gay Traitor. **Paulette:** "Girls could go to Flesh and not feel like they were being chased the second they walked in. It was about music. Let's stand on the podium, take a pill and do whatever we like. You'd meet somebody, write the name down on the back of a fag packet or a beer mat and have something to eat in the café. It was a meeting point."

Inside those doors you were safe. Outside those doors you weren't… In the early '90s you had to know how to run. You had to know how to cover up. There was danger out there, but when you got through those doors you were safe.

DJ Paulette

Previous page // Each Flesh night had a different theme, with the décor of the club following suit.

Right // Aphrodisiac winning second place in the Miss Flesh beauty pageant, accompanied by Margi Clarke, *Brookside* actress and host for the evening.

Flesh
10

Right // Just an average night at Flesh.

Flesh wasn't in an underground club somewhere, it was really exposed. Everybody wanted to go. It was the place to be. It felt like it was lifted and celebrated…

Jemima

Above // Eclectic and electric nights at Flesh.

Opposite // An audience with New York-based drag performer, Lady Bunny.

Above // 'Perverts of the world unite!' Fetish and rubber wear designers Murray and Vern hosted a 'fetish fantasy' event at Flesh. The night led to the "Fags and Slags" tour, which took place throughout 1993, with events including fashion shows in Leeds, Glasgow and London.

Opposite // Angela (of Murray and Vern) and Liz at Flesh.

Opposite // Scenes from the Murray and Vern tour, conceived and kicked off at Flesh.

The interesting thing for me with Flesh, is that I wore very little. The less I could wear the better, because I was DJing downstairs in the basement, and there was no air conditioning. The place was a sweatbox. So, every month I played, there was sweat dripping off the ceiling, rolling down the walls. The floor was like a skating rink. I was the Queen of the sequin bikini and marabou feathers. I had handcuffs, high boots, all sorts of shit going on.

DJ Paulette

Above // Fashion show from the Flesh-inspired "Fags and Slags" tour in 1993, modelled by Pam Hogg with Andy and Carolyn Blake.

Opposite // The finale of the fashion show, with models including DJ Paulette.

It was like being in the cast of some sexy '90s youth soap opera. There were so many characters, it was almost like its own TV show.

Anthony Crank

Todd Terry is a DJ and record producer.

We used to play London earlier in the day and drive out late at night to close the club. I'd usually be with three or four of my friends and a lot of the Manchester United guys. Everybody in the club had a great vibe with each other; it wasn't malicious, it was just really good fun. That was always my experience there.

People wanted to be in the booth as I mixed and played their favourite song. I remember they'd sing in my ear. There was a really powerful connection to the music inside the club and also a powerful connection between everybody who was there to experience it.

People wanted to connect any way they could. They would hand stuff up to me, notes that would say "I love you" or requests for songs, or they'd hand stuff to the bouncer, and he would walk all the way from the floor to the booth to give it to me. It got to the point where he would say "Todd, I'm not doing this shit anymore!" It was all really interesting and obscure tracks people were requesting. Sometimes I'd forget that I even had it. Back then we were only using records, so it took a lot longer to search for a track. I remember one time a girl started crying because it took me so long to find the song she wanted.

The club had its own thing going on. New York was angrier, the Haçienda had its gang moments, yes, but it was not somewhere that you had to worry about fighting all the time. You had to show your strength, sure, but it was a place to listen to good music with your friends.

I remember there was a guy that used to work at the club who would keep his leather jacket with a huge, bushy collar on all night. I'd look at him like "take off your fucking jacket, man!" because he would be dripping in sweat, but he looked great. He was this tough-looking guy with big muscles, and he wore the jacket really well. The guys seemed to over-dress more than the girls. People wanted to show they had money and that they were tough, but it didn't stop people from dancing and having a good time.

They enjoyed all types of music, I'd play records from RUN DMC and that would always go down well because I don't think it was as common to hear rap records in the club at that time. I felt like I could go anywhere with the music I played there, because the crowd was a really open-minded group of people. I felt powerful behind the decks and my mixes were slick, I would look out into the crowd and you could see that people thought it was dope.

I thought the Haçienda was going to be a forever thing like Ministry of Sound. I wanted it to live forever because the vibe was so great and it's always been one of my favourites. I don't ever think that's going to go away.

People felt good, they felt comfortable. People would travel from all over the world to come to that club. It was always a good crowd, people having fun. Even the gangsters struggled to be tough around that music. You can't fight when listening to those tracks, you have to give in and enjoy it. That's what I think the club is known for, a really good time.

I think it taught me a lot. Definitely about football and the culture of the game in the UK. I used to hang out with a lot of the Manchester players and it became a really nice family vibe. The bouncers were always so happy to see me when I was playing, too, they knew the music was going to be good that night.

I used to play a lot of my own music, alongside the Chicago house tracks, and I would test new records at the Haçienda. Some of the biggest tracks in the club at that time were "Dreams of Santa Anna" by Orange Lemon and "Can You Party" by Royal House. These were the anthems for that place. And it didn't matter if the DJ before me had already played it, they still wanted to hear me play it again.

One time I brought a drum machine with me and I was playing stuff out of that. The crowd didn't really notice, they just thought it was a record, but the people that came into the booth thought it was dope. I think I was one of the first DJs to ever do that, so it was really exciting to have that moment in the Haçienda.

It made me value my music and believe in my songs. It also taught me that singing and dancing was a really big deal to people.

Opposite // Tony Wilson with designer Ben Kelly.

I felt like I could go anywhere with the music I played there, because the crowd was a really open-minded group of people. I felt powerful behind the decks and my mixes were slick, I would look out into the crowd and you could see that people thought it was dope.

440ml

Above // Angel, a performer at Flesh.

1993-

1996

By the mid-1990s, Britain had changed, and the Haçienda, no longer setting the agenda, was keen to catch up. Although it had ignited a northern youth revolution, the club had ceased to rule the roost. Yet at the same time its industrial style and indelible cachet remained resolutely at the pinnacle of Manchester's clubbing scene. So many people testify to its impact that it seems unwarranted, to say the least, that things appeared to be grinding down. The term 'life-changing' is bandied around with recurring and serious intent, but for the generation that wasn't there at the beginning, the club remained something of a holy grail, talked about in bedrooms and playgrounds with all the magical aura of Oz.

"When I first started going to the Haçienda, it was quite moody," says the journalist Paul Flynn. "You had to work to make friends there, but it was definitely the kind of place where encounters could change lives. I remember this girl coming up to me once, quite a plump girl, with that Swing Out Sister haircut everyone had at the time. She opened her backpack and got a copy of *Lolita* out, which she gave to me and told me to go and read in the toilet. So literally, I took the book to the gents and read the first chapter. That sort of thing didn't happen in Rotters."

But by 1993 art was thrown aside, violence had escalated and guns were becoming increasingly commonplace. At this dangerous juncture, Mike Pickering swiftly vacated his DJing role, keen to pursue the soon-to-be massive music project, M People. The catalyst for departure? The time a punter asked him to play a record, at gunpoint. "That was it for me," he says sagely, "it all became too much."

"Did the Haçienda make me the person I am today? That's a tough one. I think we all contributed, and it contributed back to us. We learnt from each other. I'm really grateful to it, but I'm more grateful to the people I met there. The room that we inhabited – that brilliant, cavernous theatre – was the thing that enabled us. I always thought the Haçienda was a meeting place for creative people. Every city needs that."

What the city didn't need was the gangsters. Anyone frequenting the Haçienda at this time will testify to their unnerving presence. "I don't like to talk about specific things really," says former assistant manager Anton Razak, "but you've got guys standing in a line at the edge of the dancefloor with their hands in their pockets. You don't know what are in those pockets, or what's going on. The gangs were a law unto themselves. I was there the night when six doormen got stabbed."

Despite appalling acts of violence, the show – a slightly flagging version of what had made it so great in previous years – marched bravely on. New talent, such as Allister Whitehead, brought a fresh musical sensibility to the club, while superstar colleagues, like "son of God" Sasha and John Digweed, steered the dancefloor towards a more progressive, trance-fuelled runway that took flight with extraordinary velocity.

"It was like being at the best football match in the world, when your team scores," is how club regular Jane Golding describes these years. "What I liked about the way the Haçienda presented itself was that it was really thought out. It was all very artistic. You'd go in at the beginning of the night, and all the lights would be low. Then, when people would start to come up on their ecstasy, every white light would suddenly come on, in a blaze of glory,

06

a massive tune would drop, and everything just kicked off like a mule. I've clubbed all around the world, and honestly, there was never anywhere that could match the Haçienda. Maybe Space in Ibiza compares, but I don't think anyone's really captured that same atmosphere."

Paul Flynn is equally effusive. "The first time I walked through those butcher's curtains, it was so alien and strange, like landing on the moon," he says, with wide-eyed nostalgia. "When you think of all the other clubs in town: the dolly bird joints and student indie nights, the Haçienda was clearly something different. But as it evolved into the gangster thing, and with those queues that stretched around the block, it just became overly popular and unbearable. Suddenly, the whole world starts looking at it. It turned into a destination."

In essence, the Haçienda was youth incarnate, a young person's playpen with no responsible nanny in sight. "Very few older people went there," says Flynn. "It was very young, very pretty and it was very wasted. It was beautiful in that Northern way, where not everybody looks like a model, but they look young and fresh. People knew how to dress. Everybody knew what kind of magazines to read and what book was good and which films are out at that time. People were switched on."

Much of this, the laissez-faire approach that singled out the club from the competition, was born from the people that attended. But without doubt the club's immense scale and jaw-dropping design instilled a sense of ambition, that anything was possible within this cathedral of dreams.

"The place was a blank open space," says DJ Paulette. "That was unusual in Manchester at the time because clubs were either spit and sawdust pubs with sticky carpet, or saccharine wine bars with the worst soundtrack, playing Simply Red, Curiosity Killed the Cat and Level 42. The Haçienda was the antithesis to all the chrome and mirror pick-up joints. It wasn't a meat market, it was all about the music. Girls could go there and not feel like they were being chased the second they walked in. It was a meeting point where you'd meet like-minded individuals – your tribe. This much is true."

There was still life to be led in these penultimate years, but the general consensus remained that nothing would top the club's glory days. "Even though I loved the Haçienda, I was really upset about those dark experiences with the gangs," says Anton Razak. "After that, I didn't really care for the place too much. In fact, I stayed away."

Razak's sentiments echo what most people felt in the club's latter years. The situation with the gangs, and the unrelenting violence, was becoming untenable, but there was little prospect of hope. "Deep down, I was probably really upset, because I'd spent a lot of time there. I was saddened to hear that it closed, but I think it had to. It couldn't carry on."

"Even now if I drive past, it makes me very sad that the building has become flats," says Jane Godfrey. "I know there's not one person in that block who would have ever stood in the club. If you did, you wouldn't have bought a flat there. That would've been sacrilege."

As the decade moved on, the Haçienda resolutely failed to keep up. Genres came and went, pianos continued to bash out the chords, but most of those attending in these twilight years wouldn't know the difference between their house and their elbow. The mainstream had arrived and things would never be the same.

Left // Che Storey remembers: "After a night at the Haç, having come back from there and walked all the way to the South Trafford College of Knowledge. Mad sod. The 'drip' is most definitely the indie kid look of the day."

Opposite // Scenes from the club in the mid-'90s.

Right // Lost in the music in the middle of the dancefloor. **Jo Thornhill** remembers: "Such good times."

Did the Haçienda make me the person I am today? That's a tough one. I think we all contributed, and it contributed back to us. We learnt from each other. I'm really grateful to it, but I'm more grateful to the people I met there.

Mike Pickering

FAC51 THE HAÇIENDA

ensoniq

Opposite and above // Sub Sub featuring Melanie Williams, whose song 'Ain't No Love (Ain't No Use)' was a hit at the club. Sub Sub, who reportedly formed after a night at the Haçienda, played the club with Peter Hook appearing as guest bassist.

Noel Gallagher is a musician and was a regular at the club.

The Haçienda defines an era. At first it was a gig venue, and not a very pleasant one – I remember it being cold and empty. Acid house changed all of that.

For me, it was all about the music. That initial two or three years of acid house remains untouchable – it was magical and timeless.

I would dress the usual moody Mancunian way when I went to the Haçienda. I'm not sure that I ever took my jacket off once, no matter how hot it would get in there.

I still have friends from that era, people that I met in the club that I didn't know before. We bonded because of ecstasy, but we stayed friends because we experienced a revolution. Like old soldiers.

Noel Gallagher

Above // The Chemical Brothers performing at the club in 1995.

Opposite // The team behind the Haç: manager Ang Matthews and the bar staff.

Fac 51 The Haçienda
11-13 Whitworth Street We
FAC51
THE HAÇIENDA
STAFF
FAC51
THE HAÇIENDA
STAFF
FAC51
THE HAÇIENDA
STAFF
FAC51
THE HAÇIENDA
STAFF

Above // Comedy double act Reeves and Mortimer in the club.

Opposite // Scenes from 1990s Haçienda, including DJing from John Peel and Paula Yates, who appeared at the club to host Mr Gay UK at Flesh.

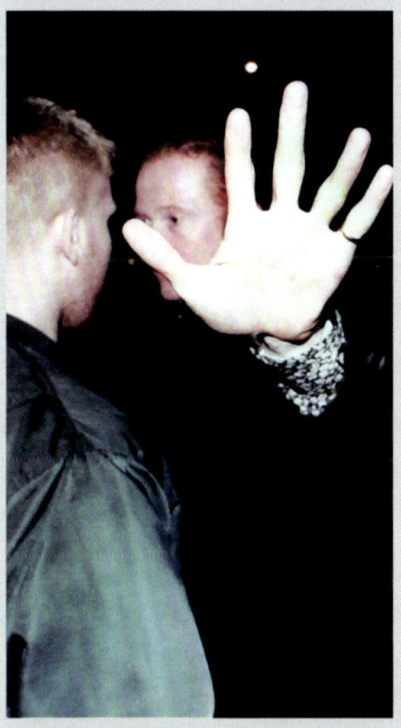

Above // As an essential part of Manchester's social scene, the club became a frequent haunt for celebrities of the 1990s.

Scully is a veteran of the Manchester music scene and was a regular at the club.

I was first introduced to the club in 1987 as a 15-year-old kid. I was aware that New Order had a link to it, which intrigued me as I loved them at time and still do to this day. My dad also knew Tony Wilson, so there was always some sort of connection.

I remember going in September 1987 for the first time, as it was just after I went to see Gary Mason fight in a bullring in Marbella, which was on 30 August 1987. The club was cold and empty, and I don't remember it filling up or getting any warmer.

The difference between the Haçienda and the few other clubs I had been to up until that point was monumental; the other clubs all required that you wore shoes, trousers and a shirt and tie. With these unquestionable rules in place, it meant most people in these clubs looked like a snide Kevin Webster or a *Bullseye* contestant – all moustaches and Krugerrand rings.

I seem to remember that, without fail, nights in these clubs would end in a fight as some nuisance with a perm got the hump because people were pointing at it, or his shiny shoes got stood on. You could also smoke hash in the Haçienda, which during my smoking days was a real plus.

One of my fondest memories of going is with a mate. We spent a fiver each – £2.50 to get in and we shared an acid tab at £5 – that's testament to the greatness of the club. There were loads of great nights, though. I'd hate to narrow it down to just one; it was a magical period.

My dress sense was quite conservative at the time. I wore Levi's denim shirts, straight-leg jeans and a Timberland moccasin leather boot. I also wore Armani jeans and a little bit of Lacoste. Nothing too crazy!

The experiences I had there have shaped every single day of my life since. When it became my regular haunt during its acid house period, I felt like I was in the centre of the universe, surrounded by people like me sharing the same moment. We all knew we were in the right place at the right time and didn't want it to end.

Club culture is great for shaping creativity and for forging friendships. I went to Ibiza for the opening night of Amnesia in the summer of 1990 to see the Happy Mondays and 808 State, and after intending on spending a fortnight there, I ended up spending months there meeting people from all over the world, having a ball and making some great friends with whom the party would continue upon our return to the Haçienda. As for the creative aspect, you only have to look at the bands, DJs, promoters and probably any talent of a certain age who passed through the club to see its importance.

I think the legacy is huge, and it's down to the foresight of Mike Pickering and his impeccable taste in music. It was his night. It was him booking the acts. It was the records he introduced us all to. Everybody else fell into line and gave us their variants to some degree. So, a big thank you there. It was all new for a reason, because he nailed it early doors. That's the legacy for me, anyway.

My memories from the club are all good. It was a magical place and a magical period in my life. It definitely shaped me as I was so young when it was my go club, it was all-consuming and took over my world, I loved every single minute of it. I thought it would last forever – it didn't, but the Haçienda will always be a bit of me.

Sadly, the good times came to an end. Despite the success of nights such as Freak (overleaf), the club closed its doors on 28 June 1997.

Manchester Evening News

Late Final

BT NORTH WEST DAILY NEWSPAPER OF THE YEAR

Monday, June 7, 1999 30p

England battle cry

Phil Neville exclusive in the M.E.N Sport pink pull-out

HACIENDA RAVE ENDS IN RIOT

■ The party's over: Police haul away one of the Hacienda ravers Picture: Eamonn Clarke

RIOT police clashed with more than 1,000 revellers outside a rave night at the former Hacienda nightclub in Manchester city centre.

BY IAN MARROW

There were 20 arrests and one policeman was injured when the "party" staged by squatters occupying the building turned nasty.

At the height of the trouble more than 70 policemen, including 20 Tactical Aid Group men in full riot gear, were called in to disperse crowds.

Officers were pelted with bricks, bottles and buckets of urine by the 1000-strong crowd outside the building and from the roof of the Hacienda.

The club, which helped build Manchester's worldwide reputation as dance scene capital of Britain, has been boarded up while negotiations continue over its future. Current plans involve turning it into luxury flats. But on Friday night squatters moved in and posted notices warning the owners GR Morris Construction that they would be prosecuted if they tried to reclaim it.

Leaflets from a group calling themselves the Okasional Cafe, who are allied to the Reclaim the Streets movement, were distributed around Manchester inviting all-comers to a free vegan meal on Saturday night.

The electricity was switched on, sound equipment and beer was brought in and the party got under way. But just after midnight huge crowds gathered outside and the police were called in and asked the squatters to leave.

Their efforts to clear the building were met with scenes of "serious disorder" in Whitworth Street West. Officers eventually dispersed the crowd outside — and started negotiating with hundreds of partygoers inside who had bar-

Turn to Page 3

Big jobs boost in £20m Tesco package

BY IAN MARROW

BRITAIN'S biggest supermarket chain Tesco is to open a new store in Stalybridge, bringing hundreds of new jobs to the town.

The £20 million deal, to build a 55,0000sq ft store on the former Delta Cable factory site off Trinity Street, was clinched this afternoon.

Developers Manchester-based CTP St James have been negotiating with Tameside Council for over two years, and the work will also include two non-food shops, a pub/restaurant, petrol station and new homes on the former industrial site.

Delighted council bosses said the deal brings the total public and private sector investment in Stalybridge over the past two years to more than £38 million — with more yet to be announced.

They point to new homes, businesses and environmental improvements which have already come to the town — and said work begins this summer to re-open the Huddersfield narrow canal.

Chairman of Stalybridge district assembly Coun Kevin Walsh said: "This is great news for the town.

SPORT FIND THE PINK PAGES AND YOU'VE FOUND THE SPORT

BUSINESS NOW IT'S ALWAYS AT THE BACK OF THE PINK PAGES

Above and opposite // Though its doors had closed, the club's anarchic spirit lived on – in the form of a rave held by people squatting in the vacant building.

RIOT IS FINAL BLOW FOR 'MOST FAMOUS NIGHTCLUB IN THE WORLD'

Hacienda's violent farewell

■ THE ENFORCERS: Seventy police, many in full riot gear, gather outside the Hacienda while, inside, a thousand squatters rave the night away

Pictures: GARY ROBERTS

BY PAUL TAYLOR

THE Hacienda stood for years as a potent symbol of all that is good and bad about Manchester.

In the 80s it was at the cutting edge of Britain's dance music revolution becoming, briefly, the most famous club in the world.

But as the 90s dawned, the party was already ending and it was merely the most famous of many clubs beset by gangs who brought violence, drug-dealing and protection rackets to Manchester's night life.

The Hacienda had been set up in 1982, funded jointly by Manchester's own rock-dance pioneers New Order and the independent Factory Records. It was the brainchild of New Order's manager Rob Gretton, who died last month aged 46. His simple reason for wanting the Hacienda was that "there was nowhere else to go" in Manchester, and his faith sustained the club through the initial five years when it made a loss.

The Hacienda's DJs were among the first in Britain to import Chicago house music and a city already famous for dour guitar rock then embraced dance rhythms too, throwing up bands such as the Stone Roses and Happy Mondays.

But in July 1989 Claire Leighton, 16, collapsed outside the club and died in hospital after taking Ecstasy. From then on the Hacienda was being feted around the world but condemned on its own doorstep.

While it was voted the Best Venue in Britain, Greater Manchester Police tried to revoke its licence, claiming it was being used for blatant drug-taking.

The city's licensing committee reprieved the club after assurances that the premises were under better control but it closed voluntarily in the face of gun-toting gangs.

Three months later it tried again but the magic had gone.

The Hacienda closed for the last time in summer 1997 with debts of £500,000.

At 8am the last ravers abandoned their squat

From Page One

-ricaded the doors. They were warned that police intended going in and at about 8am yesterday the partygoers left voluntarily.

A director of GM Morris Construction, Brian Leonard, said the building had been damaged and the owners are considering legal action. "We don't know how they got in," he said.

One of the rave organisers, who did not want to be identified, said: "There was no trouble until the police arrived."

She said the event was organised to raise cash for members of Reclaim the Streets who were arrested at a recent demonstration.

Most of those arrested for public order offences at the Hacienda have been bailed to appear on July 5 or 6.

■ Battle zone: Party's over for one raver while others try to climb into the club

£99 DEPOSIT
And From Only
£28.95 PER WEEK
UNTIL EASTER 2000
R&S REG

FIAT PUNTO 60S
5 Speed Gearbox, Rear Wash Wipe, Stereo Radio Cassette, Choice of Colour
From Only £5495
R REG From Only £4495
Plus NO payments UNTIL OCTOBER 1999
AS THE UK'S LARGEST MOTOR RETAILER OUR HUGE BUYING POWER MEANS WE CAN BUY CHEAPER AND PASS THE BENEFIT ON TO YOU. WE CAN GIVE YOU HUGE SAVINGS ON NEARLY NEW CARS.
17.5% APR
REG VARDY
MAKING CARS AFFORDABLE
CHANCELLOR LANE, MANCHESTER TEL. 0161 273 2273
ALBION WAY, SALFORD TEL. 0161 737 7833
Car shown for illustration purposes only. Written quotations on request. Licensed credit brokers. Subject to status. Customers may choose to pay weekly or monthly. Cash Price £5495. Deposit £99.00. No Payments Until October '99 Then 26 Weekly Payments @ £28.95 Followed By 221 Weekly Payments @ £32.88 Or 6 Monthly Payments @ £125.45 Followed By 51 Monthly Payments @ £141.55. Total Amount Payable £8228.25. Less £96.59 Paid By Reg Vardy. APR 17.5%.

he hacienda
must be built...
laid to rest.
R.I.P.

STELLA ARTOIS

We are EVERYWHERE
resist
21
Santana
Kirsty
STONE

For me, the Haçienda was that moment in my life where things changed forever. If it wasn't for that club, I wouldn't be the man I am stood in front of you today. It shaped me.

Bez

The L

egacy

"I only caught the end of the Haçienda," says Paul "Fletch" Fletcher. "The first time I went I was just sixteen, and it was something of an eye-opening night. Obviously, as a kid I'd never seen anything like it. But here I am, walking through those famous doors, and the first thing that hits me was the smell of poppers. Then I remember going to the toilet and there was this guy in there, projectile vomiting into one of the urinals. Glamorous? No. Exciting? Hell, yes!"

Fletch may have been late to the party, but the sights, sounds and dubious smells of the club made a lasting impression. "One of my most memorable nights was seeing Sasha and John Digweed play at Northern Exposure on a Thursday night. I remember it because I'd had a little bit of 'help' on this occasion and the music really started to make sense. After that, I was a big fan of Sasha for years. I followed him around the world. Life was sweet."

Thirty years later and this ardent fan of the Haçienda is instrumental in bringing the club back to life for a new generation. The venue may be long gone, its coals raked over in documentaries, films and the minds of clubbers of pensionable age, but its spirit marches on regardless. After a period of introspection, a time when no one really knew what to do with the brand, the Haçienda has risen, phoenix-like, from the flames – a behemoth of nightlife mythology.

"People of a certain age never got the opportunity to go there, so it's a mystical thing," he says. "When we do events at the Warehouse Project in Manchester (a venue that can pack in over 10,000 people) the demographic is anything from 18 to 70 years old. I like the idea that people are going out with their mums and dads. It's weird, but great at the same time, because those people grew up with that music and it's being passed on. I always say I love Elvis because my dad used to play it, so I've got a soft spot for him. It's nostalgic. I feel like with the Haçienda, something similar has happened. Parents bang on about house music, kids listen to it, and then the baton gets passed on."

Another surprising offshoot of the brand (resolutely a brand these days, illustrated on oven gloves the world over), is the phenomenon that is Haçienda Classical. The concept of the biggest tunes in the club's history being reimagined by an orchestra is an insane notion. But it works.

"We were always looking at different angles the club could take," says Fletch. "I started to take note of how many orchestral parts there were in dance tracks, but we didn't wanna do anything that would harm the legacy of the club. Certain people in the organisation couldn't get their heads around it, but some tracks just lent themselves well to the idea. We have the Camerata Orchestra, singers, a choir, all bringing this live element to something that's essentially just a bit of wax."

Strings of life? If all this sounds too easy, there are those who question its validity. Is the Haçienda a living breathing thing, or just a buzzword that people over-romanticise, in search of the past?

07

"I think what's good about the events they do now," says Leroy Richardson, "is that I see people that used to go to the club, customers when I was working there, and I get to meet their sons and daughters too. All they've ever heard is how good the Haçienda is, all their lives. Now they're understanding what their parents are on about."

"When we do the Haçienda club nights, there are kids there that weren't even born when the club closed," says Graeme Park. "My question is, do you play music to the people in front of you? If it's a young crowd they don't have baggage, it's easy."

"The name definitely has weight, "says Chad Jackson. "Even the university students I teach, they all know about the Haçienda and its glory years. They often ask about it, and hold it in high regard. It's a legendary thing they wish they could have been part of. The events they do now, they're big, but I rarely play old stuff. I'll put one or two choice things in there, underplayed things that people have not heard for years, but it's not about nostalgia for me."

"As long as young people don't misunderstand it, I'm cool," says Mike Pickering. "But I do think it needs a bit of a redress now and again. They sell Haçienda candles now, which smell of nothing. I think it gets a bit mad really. It's like when you walk around west London, you see a lot of posh kids wearing Joy Division t-shirts. They don't care who that is, it could be anybody on there."

"Looking back, I think it was the lunatics taking over the asylum," says Paul Flynn. "You were part of a young wave that looked pretty, knew how to take drugs, knew all the best records and are having sex for the first time, with people that you want to have sex with. It all converged into this melee of really infectious energy. Literally, we were having the time of our lives."

Of course, Tony Wilson is absolutely the incubator of it all. "Anybody with a Manchester accent of a certain age are only doing what they do now because they went to the Haçienda. Vernon Kay and Tess Daly were all over it. Had they not been there, Vernon would've been the manager of a shoe shop."

The Haçienda resolutely lives on in hearts and minds. As a cultural touchstone, it's the first thing people mention when they think of Manchester. The club, Factory Records, Joy Division, 'Blue Monday' – these are the reference points that ignite fierce debate, cherished memories and a palpable sense of belonging. French fashion house Chanel brought their runway show to the Northern Quarter in 2023, hijacking the graphics and soundtrack of the Haçienda with genuine admiration. Factory International, Manchester's ambitious new arts space, blatantly lifted its name from the musical heritage of its birthplace. What other city has such a powerful connection to a nightclub, somewhere that closed almost three decades ago? It's an umbilical cord that remains uncut.

The Haçienda is here to stay. And that's a FAC.

Above and opposite // The spirit of the Haçienda lives on in club nights and events, including one held in London's Tobacco Dock to celebrate the club's 40th birthday.

Above and opposite // Though the club holds events around the country and even the world, it brings it all back home to Manchester as well, with events including a homecoming show featuring old friends such as Ian Brown.

Haçienda
Pioneer DJ
Pioneer DJ
Pioneer DJ
Pioneer DJ

FAC51

Opposite and above // Taking its lead from the "anything goes" creative ethos of performances held at the club, the Haçienda's modern-day events span the musical spectrum, including the Haçienda Classical, which sees DJs such as Roger Sanchez performing alongside orchestras and choirs.

Left and opposite // Classical or club night, warehouse or open air, the Haç continues to bring people together to dance, share and celebrate.

Acknowledgements

To Pete, Jack, Andrea and Jess thank you for being there always to support me – you mean the world to me xx

For my Haçienda Girls – Ang Matthews, Ang Kirk, Liz Page and Ali Bell for championing my little idea – we got there in the end! Thank you so SO very much ladies x

An extra big thank you to Ang Mathews, who is a true fountain of Haçienda knowledge and as well as being an incredible woman in general is also a great friend. Thank you my lovely xx

To Carrie Kania, thank you for finding the right publisher, I'm truly grateful for the introduction to Joe at Welbeck, he's a star! (And very patient!!)

For Paul, thank you for all the help you've given me with the dates and references , I'm so happy to have got to know you after all these years! And for creating some of the most memorable nights for us all! We had the best time xx

For Kevin Cummins, Pete Walsh, Jon Shard, Eammon Clarke, Gary McClarnan, Dave Swindells, David Simms, Pete Ashworth, Elaine Constantine, Louise Rhodes and Ant Mulryan thank you for your imagery, enthusiasm and collating your archives for this project. For Alison Knight, Consalvo Pellecchia, Janet Kimber, Dave Spence, Joanne Collin, Paul O'Neill, Nick Barton, Nyree Patten, Dawn Wood, Alison Raftery, Wendy Allen, Darren Earnshaw, Jo Thornhill, Zoe Lewis, Richard Engler, Andrew Reeves, Rob Hampson, Mishelle Jordan, John Pierce, Jeff Richards, Andrew Pembroke, Paula Rice, Stella Atkinson, Mark Hoyle – thank you from the bottom of my heart for the pictures, memories and making this book possible.

To everyone who took the time and effort to send in their Haçienda memories, thank you, thank you, thank you. We were inundated with so many amazing photos and stories. We hope discovering these brought back the good days in full force!

For Bruce Mitchell, John Cooper Clarke, Phil Jones, Ian Griffiths, Irvine Welsh, Andrew O'Hagan, Rowetta, Bez, Graeme Park, Mike Pickering, MC Tunes, Melanie Williams, Mark XTC, Hewan Clarke, Todd Terry, Roger Sanchez, DJ Paulette, Kath Dermot, Luke UNA, Justin Robinson, Grandmaster Flash, Matt Squire, Pete Walsh, Graham Massey, Suddi Ravi, Paul Cons, Paul Flynn, Oscar Pinto, Michelle Kelly, Michael Richmond, Leroy Richardson, Greg Wilson, Andrew Berry, Jon Dasilva, Jon Blyther, Clint Boon, Noel Gallagher, Scully, Mani, Lee Baxter, David Hoyle, John Richmond, Murray & Vern, Elton Jackson, Ronika and Jemima, Tracey Donnelly, Suzanne, for their honest and heartfelt memories. So much love for you guys x

For Paul Tierney and Emma Davidson, thank you for setting the scene and telling the story perfectly. So proud of your work. James Anderson, thank you for giving me Paul…!

For Trevor Johnson, Che Storey and Russ for making the pages flow and managing to get so much in! Thank you x (and Frankie Stevenson, a genius in the making!!) x

For Vera Green, thank you for pulling thousands of images together and making sense of them all, it was a mammoth task done with ease. You're a star.

For Carl Bellingham for being you, we wouldn't change a thing. For Imelda Mountfield and Clare Kelly – Gorgeous Girls, Beautiful Souls.

For Guy Williams, Gina Love & Daniella B (Beehive_n_Love), Steve Caton, Andy Fisher, Matt Ryan, Diane Marsh, Alison Walsh, Jane Godly, Michael Duignan, Anthony Crank, Andy Polaris, James Anderson, Chad Jackson, Peter Chadwick, Alex Sharky, Roy Brown, Anton Razak, David Gonzalvo, Guy Ainsworth, Annabella Lwin, Neil Arthor, Burning Spear, Jane Casey. Thank you for the stories both humorous and moving.

Mr Paul Fletcher, for your continued hard work and forward thinking. Thank you darling for keeping the memories alive x

And lastly, to Mr James Masters. This one's for you my lovely. Our right hand man who was always the epitome of style and sophistication.

Love Always Bex x x x

Photography credits

The author and publishers would like to thank the following sources for their kind permission to reproduce the pictures in this book.

Wendy Allen 57 (top right, bottom right); Stella Atkinson and Paul O'Neill 184, 185 (top left, bottom left, bottom right), 190, 191 (middle, bottom); Avalon/Getty Images 169; @beezerphotos 78, 83, 84, 85, 86–87; John Blyther (Tracy) 58; Clint Boon 137; Paula Bowden 201; Jeremychaplin.com 231, 232, 234, 235; Eamonn Clarke 257, 258, 259, 266, 267, 268–269; Joanne Collin 210 (left); Andre Csillag/Shutterstock 194; Kevin Cummins 14–15, 18, 20, 21, 24–25, 36–37, 38, 39, 41, 42 (top right, bottom), 49, 50, 61, 62, 63, 64–65, 68, 69, 71, 80, 98–99, 118–119, 131, 132, 134, 135, 149, 158, 160, 161, 163, 164–165, 192–193, 288; Ann Dinan 22; From the collection of Darren Earnshaw 40, 42 (top left), 43, 44 (top left), 51, 59, 73 (left top, middle, bottom), 186; Mike Forster/ANL/Shutterstock 123; Richard Engler 56, 57 (top left), 70; Len Grant Photography / Alamy Stock Photo 6, 130; Karen Haze 73 (bottom right); Dylan Hoo 280 (bottom left, bottom right); Clive Hunte/Redferns/Getty Images 247 (bottom left, top right); Niels van Iperen/Getty Images 67; Elton Jackson 210 (right); Suzanne Jackson 147 (bottom right); By Johnson/Panas © Trevor Johnson 103–106 Zumbar ID/print, 133, 148, 198–199, 246 (bottom); Michelle Jordan 73 (top right); Michelle Kelly 200; Janet Kimber 182, 183, 185 (left middle, top right), 187, 188, 189; Jack Kirwin, JK Photography 272–273; Alison Knight 29; Dominic Lowe and Phil Morris 57 (bottom left); Manchester Digital Music Archive 44 (bottom left), 45; The Manchester Evening News 266–267; Mani 31; Gary McClarnan 102, 103, 105, 110, 111 (right), 112, 113, 152, 157, 204; Ant Mulryan 250, 251; Photographs courtesy Omega Auctions 26–27, 28, 48, 198–199; Gemma Parker 283 (bottom right), 284 (top, bottom); Photoshot / TopFoto 142–143, 253; Phil Portus / Alamy Stock Photo 101; Jeff Richards 23;John Richmond 30; Louise Rhodes 2;Ronika 197; Consalvo Pellecchia 202, 203;John Pierce 190 (top right), 247 (top left, bottom right); Danny Sargeant 276, 280 (top), 281, 283 (top, bottom left); Frans Schellekens/Redferns/Getty Images 175; Jon Shard 12–13, 178 179, 208, 209 (bottom), 211, 212, 213, 214 215, 216, 217, 218, 219, 220–221, 223, 224, 225, 226, 227, 228, 229, 237, 264–265; Dominic Simpson 277, 278–279, 282, 284 (middle), 285; Dave Spence 88 (left); Che Storey 246 (top); Dave Swindells 11, 94, 95, 96, 97, 128, 129, 138 (top, bottom), 139, 140, 141; Jo Thornhill 248–249;Dawn Tivendale (147 (top, bottom left);Trinity Mirror / Mirrorpix / Alamy Stock Photo 146 (bottom); Peter J Walsh 9, 34, 52–53, 89, 91, 92–93, 108–109, 116, 117, 122, 126, 127, 145, 146 (top), 155, 166, 167, 170, 172, 173, 238, 239, 240, 241, 242–243, 254, 255, 256, 260–261, 263; Dave Wilson 74–75, 104, 107

The Haçienda name and logo copyright © 2024 Three Little Pigs Limited
Foreword © 2024 Peter Hook
Introductory text © 2024 Paul Tierney
Interview text © Original copyright owners
Design and layout © Carlton Books Ltd

First published in 2024 by Welbeck
An Imprint of HEADLINE PUBLISHING GROUP

1

Apart from any use permitted under UK copyright law, this publication may only be reproduced, stored, or transmitted, in any form, or by any means, with prior permission in writing of the publishers or, in the case of reprographic production, in accordance with the terms of licences issued by the Copyright Licensing Agency.

Cataloguing in Publication Data is available from the British Library

ISBN 978-1-80279-768-8

Printed and bound in China

MIX
Paper | Supporting responsible forestry
FSC® C104740

Publisher: Joe Cottington
Design: Russell Knowles
Production: Rachel Burgess

Headline's policy is to use papers that are natural, renewable and recyclable products and made from wood grown in well-managed forests and other controlled sources. The logging and manufacturing processes are expected to conform to the environmental regulations of the country of origin.

HEADLINE PUBLISHING GROUP
An Hachette UK Company
Carmelite House
50 Victoria Embankment
London EC4Y 0DZ

www.headline.co.uk
www.hachette.co.uk